Dotcons

Dotcons

Con games, Fraud, and Deceit on the Internet

James T. Thomes

Writers Club Press
San Jose New York Lincoln Shanghai

Dotcons
Con games, Fraud & Deceit on the Internet

Writers Club Press
an imprint of iUniverse.com, Inc.

For information address:
iUniverse.com, Inc.
5220 S 16th, Ste. 200
Lincoln, NE 68512
www.iuniverse.com

ISBN: 0-595-14835-2

Printed in the United States of America

CONTENTS

FOREWORD

The rapid evolution of e-commerce on the Internet has outpaced our laws to regulate it! The Federal Trade Commission recently reported over 500 complaints a day about illegitimate businesses in the U.S. Internet sites are setting up off-shore, out of the jurisdiction of the laws of civilized countries, so they can bilk you without fear of legal recourse. Legitimate stocks are manipulated by e-traders, and Dotcom stocks with questionable business plans are fetching billions from eager investors. Illegitimate one-man shops are masquerading as established businesses, taking your credit card, and then disappearing into cyberspace with little or no chance of apprehension.

Violation of your privacy has become the norm while doing business on the Internet. The simple focus groups, surveys, and telephone polls that were annoying in the past have been replaced by monolithic data engines scanning websites, chatrooms, bulletin boards and e-mail for your private financial data, choices, thoughts, and opinions–selling it to anyone—with no laws to protect you.

As legitimate businesses have rushed to offer online services to an eager public, so too have some individual entrepreneurs stretched the limits of ethics, common-sense, and the law—while the fast pace and anonymity of business transactions have provided attractive opportunities for fraud. Modern versions of old-fashioned confidence games are appearing every day, and as these instances of fraud and deceit become more visible, consumers are becoming more skeptical.

As the Internet grows in popularity, this skepticism is healthy. It discourages criminals, drives government agencies to direct their efforts towards this new threat, and stimulates new technology to improve the safety of the Internet for those using it. Knowledge is power. The more we understand fraud, the better we can protect ourselves from it, and the sooner we can rid ourselves of it.

FRAUD ON THE INTERNET

In September of 2000, a 23 year old man was arrested by the FBI for a fraud perpetrated over the Internet when he spread a bogus e-mail message to an Internet investment company about a hotly traded company. He made over a quarter-million dollars in fifteen minutes.

E-commerce promises to be the next great commercial frontier, once we learn how to do it! The Internet has been around for almost two decades, but commercial usage has only been encouraged in the last five years. The transition from a non-profit system for academic and scientific endeavors to a business enterprise has not been without turbulence.

As new entrepreneurs enter the field and expand the possibilities for business and the consumer, they are stretching the limits of our laws. Like the Wild West in the early 20th Century, this new electronic frontier of the 21st has its share of snake-oil salesmen and confidence artists. Like any grand enterprise, the Dot-com businesses feature a certain number of confidence games, fraud, and deceit—"Dotcons".

- Violation of privacy has been institutionalized as a fundamental aspect of the business model for Internet advertising.
- Identity theft has been simplified and automated so that even a novice can acquire enough personal data about you to defraud you and drive you into bankruptcy.

- Bulletin boards, chatrooms and discussion groups are used by new Internet firms to gather your most private information, thoughts, and intentions about your financial and physical health.
- Stocks in fraudulent Internet companies have replaced gold mines, oil wells, pyramid schemes, and snake oil as the scam of choice for hundreds of well-financed online "brokers."
- Illegal franchising and business opportunities have proliferated to the point that the FTC receives over 500 complaints a day.
- Telephone schemes have been automated to the point that you can be automatically routed to a long-distance 900 number while you are surfing the Internet.
- Unscrupulous sellers at auction sites are selling counterfeit goods with little fear of legal recourse.
- Unsolicited e-mail has replaced the letter bomb. Open an attachment and destroy your computer, credit rating, or your business.
- Prestigious Internet sites operate off-shore, out of the jurisdiction of the laws of civilized countries, so they can bilk millions of people with no fear of prosecution.
- Computer stores and malls appear with astounding offers and discounts for expensive products that are never shipped.
- Advance Fees are collected for illegal university degrees, identification cards, licenses, credit repair, credit cards, loans, divorces, Social Security cards and pirated software—but the products are never delivered.

Internet Fraud Complaint Center

The Internet Fraud Complaint Center (IFCC) is a partnership between the Federal Bureau of Investigation (FBI) and the National White Collar Crime Center (NW3C) that was recently established to address fraud committed over the Internet. For victims of Internet fraud, IFCC provides a convenient and easy-to-use reporting mechanism that alerts authorities of a suspected criminal or civil violation. For law enforcement and regulatory agencies at all levels, IFCC offers a central repository for complaints related to Internet fraud, works to quantify fraud patterns, and provides timely statistical data of current fraud trends. If you encounter any of the confidence games, fraud, or illegal actions mentioned in this book, you are encouraged to contact the IFCC at www.ifcc.gov.

EVOLUTION OF THE INTERNET

The Internet traces its roots back to the Cold War, where it was first conceived as a communication system operated by the government that would allow us to control our military forces after a nuclear attack. Since then it has evolved into a commercial system operated by its users.

Thirty years ago, the General Staff of the Strategic Air Command was concerned with a global problem—how we were going to command our forces after a Soviet nuclear attack. At the time, the Department of Defense subscribed to a strategy that seems quite silly in retrospect–Mutually Assured Destruction or MAD. This called for us to show the Russians that it would be folly to attack us, because we would survive any first strike and retaliate with a vengeance that would ensure their destruction.

The requirement of the strategy was to develop a command and control system that would survive a nuclear attack and allow us to communicate to our bases and missile sites. The system we had at the time was too vulnerable. Power was concentrated in a few large military headquarters, and taking out one or two of the central facilities would shut everybody down.

The Department of Defense handed the problem to a non-profit civilian research agency who proposed a "decentralized" system consisting of hundreds of computers that would offer almost an infinite number of alternatives for the transmission of messages. A weblike system like this would have no centralized points that would be vulnerable to enemy attack—just thousands of nodes that were able to transmit to each other. If any node was knocked out, the messages would automatically be rerouted.

This redundancy would "bulletproof" the system. All the nodes in the network would do the same thing. Each could originate, pass, and receive messages. The messages themselves would be divided into packets. That way, if one computer was knocked out in the middle of a message, another would merely take over.

The idea had great appeal to other branches of the federal government as well as the Defense Department. After all, if we were to have a nation worth fighting for, we would have to reconstitute our communities into cities, our cities into states, and our states back into the nation. A communications system owned and operated by the federal government. *The Internet was never designed for commercial usage.*

The Seventies

In 1969, the Advanced Research Projects Agency funded the development of a test-bed to prove the concept by connecting high-speed supercomputers in universities that were being used for basic research. The first contract was awarded to UCLA. They called it the ARPANET.

Academia was eager to develop and use the new technology. When UCLA got it up and running, the Department of Defense linked more computers at other universities and research centers. The non-profit, government-owned system was popular with students and teachers alike. They all had their own personal addresses for electronic mail and were using the ARPANET for person-to-person communication. Scientists and researchers shared computer facilities to collaborate on projects. Students traded notes and protested the war.

The Department of Defense sponsors were pleased with the technological progress, but alarmed by its usage. *Academia had turned the non-profit communications system funded for strategic nuclear deterrence into an electronic post office!*

The Eighties

The Department of Defense continued to fund the ARPANET as it grew through the next decade of the Cold War. It grew quickly because the flexible redundancy that was required to operate in wartime made it easy to add new users during peacetime. The system used standard "packets of information", and any computer that could be programmed to handle a packet was free to join.

The Department of Defense continued to own and operate the system until 1989, but it was never used for the purpose it was intended, strategic command and control. The easy access to the ARPANET was it's greatest strength in a metamorphosis to civilian use, but a weakness to the military. *The decentralized system was, and remains, fundamentally ill-suited for secure data transmission.* Anybody can gain access to the packets of data, decode them if they are encrypted, and then use the information to put our military forces at risk.

Concerned with both the lack of security and the usage of the system, the military handed control to a civilian government agency—the National Science Foundation, who operated it as a non-profit resource for the government and academia. Areas of common interest were devised to categorize different kinds of users. Government users were ".gov", the military ".mil", other non-profit organizations were ".org". Networks among these users were ".net".

Although commercial use was not envisioned at the time, IBM, Unisys, and some other government contractors involved with the system suggested a ".com" for commercial users.

The new system was appealing to all, and in a symbiotic fashion, the more people that joined the non-profit system, the better it got. E-mail programs, mailing lists, search engines, editors, and then browsers—all eventually found their way to archives that could be downloaded at no charge by anybody with access to the net.

The Nineties

As the Internet continued to grow, entrepreneurs saw a promising new medium for the conduct of world-wide business and chafed at the restrictions on commercial usage.

Yielding to the demand of the commercial marketplace, the government allowed commercial business to operate on the Internet in 1991. By 1993 there were more ".com" commercial web-sites than all the other non-profit domains combined. Two years after that, the federal government stopped funding the Internet–leaving it to be managed by the participants. Academics vied for power with the business world–and lost. By 1996 there were over 10,000,000 people conducting business on the Internet.

Today

The Internet is still managed by its users–millions of them—*and when everybody is in charge, nobody is in charge.* There are federal laws that apply to the Internet, but unlike the Postal Service, which is run by the federal government, there are no regulations covering how the Internet is to be operated.

This lack of government control is a double-edged sword. On one hand it has provided a free and open medium for the explosive growth characteristic of a free market; on the other hand, it has created new opportunities to perpetrate crimes without fear of traditional law enforcement.

Like the con artists with fake mustaches in the Western Frontier, Dotcon artists with computers in the Electronic Frontier find the same trusting public to exploit. This has resulted in a flood of complaints to the state and federal governmental agencies tasked with making and enforcing laws to protect us.

Today the Internet has realized its potential as an effective new business medium. federal, state, and non-profit organizations seem committed to developing the new laws, ethics, business practices and the means to enforce them to make a safe, honest environment for the conduct of world-wide commerce. In the meantime, e-buyer beware.

INVADING PRIVACY FOR PROFIT

In a recent federal prosecution, the defendants allegedly obtained the names and Social Security numbers of 100 military officers from a web-site, then successfully used them to apply for credit cards on the Internet.

If you've ever entered your residence, birth date, salary, race, income from other sources, mother's maiden name, TV preferences, religious affiliation, marital status, the names and ages of your children, or any other minute detail of your life, you can be sure that this information is going to be sold to lots and lots of people–over and over again–some good, some bad.

If you've ever bid in an online auction, placed a bet at an online casino, or made a comment in anger at a chatroom, this too will soon be part of your record. There are companies with millions of dollars in capital setting out to collect and sell this information

"Why would they do that? Isn't that illegal?" Hell no! That's their business! Your name, e-mail address, and personal data are their stock in trade. Data about you and me are the currency of the Information Age. Selling this data is a fundamental aspect of doing business on the Internet. The economics are simple, quite honest, and perfectly legal. It's not rocket science. It's just simple math.

Revenue = Value of Information X Target Market X Usage

Are you twenty-five and stuck with a college loan for your Computer Science degree? Wish you were rich like your old man? The answer is simple: set up a web-site, sell advertising space, and collect a lot of data about a lot of wealthy people. Then sell this information.

The Value of Information

Today, in the Information Age, you can assume that every bit of information about you has some value to somebody trying to sell you something on the Internet. Your e-mail address might be worth a half-cent to somebody who is just contacting you in the blind. Add your name for somebody who wants to call you by name and get past any filter you might have to screen him out–another penny. Your address and phone number for those people who want to follow up with a call or brochure? Maybe another half-cent. Your birth date, sex, religious preference, interests, political affiliation–everything has a value to somebody, especially when they put it together. How about your social-security number or credit card? Big time! Might be worth a lot to some people–all according to how much you're worth and what they want to do with it.

Mining the Market–Mass Privacide

Big revenues on the Internet depend upon being able to access a large database of people by specific characteristics. For example, a list of e-mail addresses for a couple million people over the age of sixty would be valuable to a company selling an unproved herbal cure for arthritis. A list of a million people over sixty who asked questions about arthritis would be even more valuable. And a list of a million people over sixty with arthritis who visited sites for herbal cures might be even more valuable. The trick is to collect the list and use all the resources of the Internet to provide the most detailed information possible on everybody on the list. This used to be a tedious, laborious job—even with computers. The Internet makes it easy.

New Internet companies have sprung up offering tools and services for "Data Mining". To the casual user, this term brings up images of hardworking miners with picks and shovels diligently battling nature to earn a living wage from the earth. It's not. It's new technology that is focused on the exploitation of the free and unlimited access of the Internet.

Data mining companies capture your personal information from many different sources on the Internet—sources that you would not expect to reveal this information. Skeptics see data-mining tools as the ultimate weapon in the invasion of privacy, *because the fundamental nature of the Internet provides a fertile field for their exploitation.*

Packets of data flowing freely from site to site make it theoretically possible for anybody, anywhere, to gain access to any information if they use the right combination of software and hardware. The hardware is already here on your kid's desk; the software is coming.

Newsgroups

Tapping of newsgroups and open discussions for commercial purposes was one of the first gross exploitations of the Internet. Newsgroups are useful and accessible to everybody. No one would believe they could become the source for a sophisticated worldwide database containing your casual thoughts and observations. Your local ISP can't protect you, nor can the "Privacy Policies" overstated by major net services. When you enter private information into your computer, your message is spread worldwide by the "Usenet" of the Internet in a matter of hours. Everything you've entered can be catalogued, analyzed, evaluated, and compared with others by somebody with the resources to tap into it.

Collecting Information at web-sites

Web pages were the first source of data. Software has existed for years that can query search engines pages with the word "Ford" in it and assemble a list of "Ford" web pages. This software has now been advanced to grab the e-mail addresses on those pages for a "targeted" list of people with a presumed interest in Fords. That means if your e-mail name is listed on any web page anywhere, it can theoretically be captured by these computer programs.

The Dot-com companies just set up a web-site with something of interest to different kinds of people, advertise it on TV, and wait for people to click on it. They might offer free E-mail service or Internet access, or prizes of some kind—a free vacation to Las Vegas, Hawaii, Disney World. All you have to do is click on it, and they've got your e-mail address. Then when you fill out the "registration form" they've got the rest of your personal data.

Cookies

Once you've visited their web-site, they drop a little file on your hard drive called a "Cookie" to keep track of your personal data. Each time you visit, they can retrieve that cookie and know what you click on, what you search for, what you bid on, and soon–what you say in chatrooms, discussion groups, and e-mail. When you click on insurance, it knows you interested in a policy. When you click on Prozac, it knows you're depressed, and when you click on Funeral arrangements...it knows the advertiser better get back to you soon.

Chatrooms

Chatrooms are the most recent source of confidential information. Because they are executed with interactive web pages, they may be downloaded and scanned by anybody who can gain access to the web-site. New Internet companies have raised billions of dollars in capital with the fundamental purpose of downloading this information, scanning it, storing it in a database, and either selling it to advertisers or using it themselves.

Carnivore

Carnivore is the name of the computer program used by the FBI to do this. It's a black box that is planted in an ISP under the authority of a search warrant to tap e-mails going to and from specific addresses. It sounds sophisticated. It's really not. In fact, it's not nearly as dangerous to your privacy as the commercial software programs we've discussed. But the concept of operation is identical.

The FBI claims that Carnivore works by screening packets of information flowing in and out of the ISP for the address of the sender, recipient, and most probably the copies. These messages are intercepted and probably copied to FBI Headquarters in West Virginia. They deny looking at anybody else's e-mail for which they do not have a warrant—even though it is very difficult for them to avoid doing so.

The Attorney General has assured us that this is all perfectly legal and necessary to catch criminals, but if Big Brother taps "Simpleton@aol.com" sending a message to "CoolDude@msn.com" that says "The FBI can't find their ass with both hands." What do you think life will be like for the two youngsters in the future? Regardless of whether or not they commit a crime, they'll certainly be under routine surveillance? Does this sound intrusive?

Echelon

Compared to "Echelon", Carnivore's a toy. "Echelon" is the name of a world-wide surveillance system that has been developed by a group of English-speaking nations to intercept all electronic messages that are transmitted in the atmosphere—radio, television, and of course, any telephone, fax, or Internet data that is not sent over a cable. (Although even that is suspect). According to "60 Minutes," Echelon has been around for sometime, but the federal government will not admit to its existence. No one really knows exactly how it works, but a Freshman Computer Science student could surmise that the advent of the Internet must have been met with jubilation and glee by those tasked with interpreting the zillions of bits that are floating around in the ether. They used to have to listen carefully to telephone conversations in order to extract information. Now they simply have to feed the data through a computer and look for keywords, phrases, or names.

Unlike Carnivore, which is supposed to go after a specific e-mail name like a laser, Echelon is more like a gold miner, it gathers massive scoops of bits, and then sifts them through a filter looking for words of interest to one or more of the sponsoring nations. Theoretically the system is used to look for words associated with terrorist threats, but of course, it could be used for any purpose.

You should not assume that Echelon is dangerous because it is now being used to spy on criminals. You should assume it is dangerous because it could soon be used to spy on *you*.

Should you be concerned?

The Federal Government is developing powerful new systems to catch criminals. At the same time, they are making more activities on the net a crime. It seems axiomatic that the confluence of the two is aimed at a massive federal surveillance of the Internet. Sounds scary. How dangerous is it? Not nearly so bad as the commercial systems that are being used right now. At least the Federal Government pretends to be concerned about our privacy.

The new Internet businesses collecting data are founded on the basis that you don't want privacy. How many people are they gathering information on? Check the counter at the bottom of a popular web-site and see for yourself. Even small sites have hundreds of thousands of "hits". Then read their privacy statements clearly–if they have one. They state that information about you will be collected and retained in a database *unless specifically stated otherwise*.

For example, click on "Prozac.com", and your next job interviewer will think your depressed. Click a couple times on an adult site; you're a pervert. Enter "Hepatitis" into a search engine; you're a bad risk. And visit "Cybercasino.com"; you'll get a knock on the door. Does this upset you? Big Brother would say you've got something to hide. Thomas Jefferson would say you have a right to freedom from unnecessary searches. The government and the information companies would say they have no intention of doing this.

The large information-gathering monoliths generate their revenue by selling data about you. The y claim that personal privacy is important to them, and that anyone can choose not to have his personal data disclosed. Ask yourself, what would happen to their revenues if everybody did?

COOKIES

Cookies store personal information you enter and data transmitted by the website to your hard disk so that the information might accessed later The acquisition, storage, and subsequent dissemination of this data is done without your knowledge or consent.

Cookies were originally intended to retain semi-permanent records of information you enter so that they can be used by another web page. They are useful when online shopping. They keep track of what you have purchased as you go from web page to web page. Some can even resume your shopping trip should you be interrupted. They are also used to personalize a website. When you sign on, they call you by name, start where you left off, and use your preferences.

Cookies are text-files. The first part of the cookie is your login name, and the rest is used to generate a profile of where you go and where you click. Web servers automatically gain access to your cookies whenever you establish a connection to them by visiting their site.

The access by any website to files which contain data you may want to keep private is a fundamental weakness of the Internet that is exploited by the new technology of data-mining. Theoretically only the "domain" which set the cookie can retrieve it. The problem is that Internet companies have been established and heavily capitalized to retrieve and correlate this information, thereby establishing a broad ".net" domain that includes their clients as ".com" sites. Right now, cookies contain mostly navigational data, but there is no reason why they could not contain information from any of your personal files.

These few visionary marketing companies have established joint marketing agreements with thousands of clients to collect this information without your specific knowledge and routinely share it in a conspiracy to compromise your privacy.

Consuming Cookies

Consuming too many cookies might make you sick! You can stop eating them if you want. Unfortunately, many legitimate web-sites need them to work smoothly, while others use them primarily to gain information about you. Which are which? You can't tell.

Although each individual cookie may be encoded and used for good purpose by the website you have chosen, they can, nevertheless, be retrieved, recorded, and decoded by another that you happen upon while surfing—with all of this information being correlated by one or two information conglomerates. If this bothers you, as it does me, there are some logical steps you can take to limit the effect of consuming cookies.

Cookie Warnings

You can set your browser to tell you when you're about to get a cookie, and to give you the option of refusing it. This slows down your browsing somewhat, but it is an excellent way to find out who is collecting what information about you. Check the "Help" function of your browser for "Warn before accepting cookies".

The Cookie Jar

All websites need a standard place to store cookies on your computer. Windows makes this easy with a folder entitled "\Windows\Cookies ".

Normally you should be able to find most of the information that is being stored about you in this directory. The files are all in text format; although each cookie-maker has his or her own symbols to allow them to be read by computer They might seem like garbage at first glance, but if you look through them for a while, you'll see some of the places you've visited, the searches you've done, and the data you've entered. As the Internet grows and more people can profit by learning more and more about you, these cookie files will grow larger and larger.

Eliminating Cookies

Reading your cookies might give you the incentive to delete them. You can if you want, but it might be better to "Crunch" them as described below. If you simply delete a cookie, the website thinks you're a new user when you sign on again and asks you to enter whatever information it uses to guide your around the site (or in the case of the illegitimate Dotcon, the information it needs to defraud you or sell your data to someone else). You can run, but you can't hide on the Internet.

Crunching Cookies

You can slow down your pursuers though. One gigantic speed bump is to corrupt their cookie files by making it impossible for them to record information. A good way to do this is to delete all the contents of the file after you've finished reading it and then mark the file as read-only. This way the invading program gets nothing from the empty file–and can't add anything. If you don't like what you're seeing, or the same site appears all over some of the files, you might want to stop the invasion of your privacy.

Signing back on.

If you crunch or delete your cookies, you'll probably have to re-enter some information the next time you visit your favorite sites, because even legitimate ones use cookies to guide you around the site.

If you haven't crunched the cookies, when you do re-enter the information the website will make new ones, and you can expect that it will be used on the Internet with neither your knowledge or permission.

If you have crunched the cookies, the site will not be able to make new ones and you may be some difficulty navigating that site. If the degraded functionality bothers you, don't be alarmed. Just go back and just delete the empty file altogether.

Cookies on the Menu–Step by Step.

1. Go to the directory, folder, or file(s) on your computer that holds the cookies.. Older versions of Internet Explorer had a single file called "cookies.txt". Newer versions have a group of different files in a directory entitled "\Windows\Cookies."

2. Start "Notepad", and browse to the directory you found and open the file.

3. Read through the information, and decide whether you want to leave the file as it is, delete it so that you will be able to control the new information it handles, or crunch the file, so that it is totally inoperative.

    • To keep the file as its, just "Close it". All the functionality will be preserved and the website will continue to operate normally.

    • To start over with new information, "Close the file", select "Open" from the menu and when the files appear, delete the one you just read. This will indicate to the legitimate website that you are a new user, and you will be aware of the data you enter.

    • If you want to stop the release of specific data that is found in a cookie, you can corrupt the cookie forever by first marking the entire text, deleting it, and then saving it. Then set its attributes to read-only, hidden and system. When you log

onto the offending site, it cannot read anything, write anything, or give you a new one.

Advertising on the Internet

"Over 17,000 people will see your message every day—more than a half-million new customers every month!"

The Internet evolved from a small, non-commercial user base, and early efforts to charge for advertising were clumsy at best. As late as 1990, many companies were unwilling to advertise on the Internet, because they were unsure of how to do it. The first attempts at selling advertising space used the model of the electronic media, but this was soon replaced by a print media analogy: a rectangular ad that reaches a given amount of people. The advertisement, called a banner, has now become a standard .

Banners

Banners come in different sizes and shapes like newspaper and magazine ads, but the banner has an important edge over media. When you click on a banner, you are transported directly to the destination chosen by the advertiser. Cognitive advertising works best when information is transferred interactively to the recipient.

Different banners can be programmed to go the same place, or the same banner can be programmed to go to different places. *This flexibility is a powerful tool in the hands of marketers, for they will be aware of your predisposition when you arrive at the destination.* They know where you came from, and where you're going.

The "full banner" is half the width of the browser window and about an eighth the height. There are also half-banners, vertical banners, banners with indexes, and smaller ads known as buttons. Pricing varies by the size, shape, and positioning.

Positioning

When an advertiser purchases a full banner, it will normally be the only advertisement on the page, but some sites may display two full banners, one at the top and the other at the bottom. Like print media, these positions are called the "top fold" and "bottom fold" of the page. Positioning on the bottom fold on a some web pages may be unfavorable, because the entire page is frequently not seen by a user as he surfs through the net. You're sure to notice a banner on the "top fold", but you may never see the banner on the "bottom fold" unless you stop and scroll down the page for some reason.

Impressions

Impressions are analogous to "circulation" in the print media; that is, they measure the number of people who are exposed to the advertisement. Each time a web page is accessed by a browser, the host computer registers a "hit". If a banner appears on that page, an assumption is made that the viewer saw it; thereby registering an impression.

Banners are sold by "Cost Per Impressions" or CPM. This is the fee charged for every thousand impressions (The "M" comes from the Roman numeral for 1,000). An $18 CPM would cost $18 for each thousand times a page is selected. CPM ranges from $1 to more than $200 CPM for sites selling high value items. Most larger sites claim traffic of 10,000 or more visitors with a rate from $25 to $100 per 1,000 presentations of the ad.

Targeting

Have you ever had an insurance agent show up at your door with a policy that had your annual income already filled in? Ever gotten a call from a company offering you credit card protection after you've just reported your card stolen. Received any e-mails or letters lately that refer to your age, your kids, where you live, or how you vote. Gotten any that talk about your arthritis, your recent depression, your suicidal tendencies, or your sexual fantasies? If not, you will.

The key to successful advertising on the Internet is picking web-sites and e-mails for people who are interested in your message. And that means they have to know what you are interested in. Until recently, this targeting was limited to keeping track of information that you *voluntarily* entered into web-sites, but the latest wave of information companies are surreptitiously doing this by dropping "cookies" on your hard disk. Once they know that information they can sell it to advertisers eager to target their banner ads.

The latest ploy to intrusively contact you is called "Re-targeting". They know when you visit a web-site of one their clients, so they automatically bring up a small ad "reminding" you when you visit other sites. It's like changing the channel on your TV every once in a while without your consent. It's surprising when you see it happen!

Hand-offs to Tele-marketers

Sick of people calling you at dinner? Wonder how they got your phone number? Well, enter it on the Internet at work, and by the time you get home it will have been sold to a telemarketer. One Dot-com company proposes to do this in real time. As soon as you click on a site of one of their clients, they will sell your phone number as a "hot lead!" Just think, you'll soon have the privilege of getting a few dozen unsolicited phone calls as soon as you sign off the Net.

The Dot-com Phenomenon

Your Internet stock soared and then plummeted a year later when the earnings report came in. Like mass hypnosis, experienced investors ignored the fundamentals of the marketplace and climbed on board the roller coaster. Some got rich; others stayed too long. What were they thinking of when they bid an Internet bookseller to a capital value of IBM? What happened?

The advertising revenues forecast by the Internet were an illusion. Investors dreamed of getting in on a new advertising medium that was going to be as big as television someday. But the Internet isn't television, and many people simply ignore the banner ads. Some of this was an honest mistake. Another was a flat-out con.

Hyped Impressions

Recall that banner advertising is sold by CPM, cost per thousand impressions. An impression, or "hit" happens each time a web page is called up with the banner on it. Web pages registering a million hits per month charge a hundred times more than Web pages with a hundred-thousand hits per month. *The problem is that these "hits" can be easily faked.* As a matter of fact, in the language of the Dotcon artist, "Hits" means "How Idiots Track Success".

Check the counter at the bottom of a web-site. Now click "Refresh" at the top of your browser. The number went up. Easy to do wasn't it. This should tell you something. It should have told the investors in Dot-com stocks something too. *If you want to pump up the value of an Internet stock, hire a Dotcon artist to hype the hits.* He can sign on with a battery of computers and run a simple computer program that artificially simulates different users looking at the page. It's possible to generate thousands of hits per hour, and millions per month. But the hits aren't real people. They don't buy anything.

Advertising Metrics

Although the computer screen looked like a television screen to advertisers, efforts to sell Internet advertising using the metrics of electronic media didn't work because the TV picture filled the whole screen for a specific amount of time. Print media was seen a better analogy: a rectangular ad that reaches a given amount of people. The advertisement, called a banner, is the standard advertising metric of the Internet.

Some advertisers pulled out when banner advertising proved to be less effective than projected. Others were more patient. Because CPM wasn't correlated to sales like "circulation" of the print media, they demanded more proof of new "eyeballs" seeing the ad before they would try again.

The Web companies selling banner space countered with a new metric—"Cost per Click-through", a more accurate measure of the effectiveness of the banner. CPC is purported to be less susceptible to misrepresentation.

The software development companies countered with new programs with more sophisticated tracking capabilities for the advertiser. These new programs provide more data, trends, summaries and analyses about the hit. They purport to allow the potential advertiser to screen out these obvious ploys and get a true picture of the popularity of the site. As this is being written, "hackers" are already developing new ways to "hype" these new metrics.

The Result

Although banner advertising has great potential. It is not equivalent to radio or television. Research shows that information received in an emotional setting is more reliably remembered by the recipient, and there is little emotion involved in clicking a mouse! The Dotcom phenomenon never reached expectations because the projected sales of the Dot-com start-ups never materialized. The number of people visiting the web-sites were exaggerated and the effectiveness of the banner ads was oversold.

IDENTITY THEFT

The first indictment under the terms of the Identity theft and Assumption Deterrence Act of 1998 occurred in early 1999. A woman was apprehended for obtaining names, addresses, and Social Security numbers from a web-site and using them to apply for a series of car loans over the Internet.

Identity theft is the transfer or use of a means of identification of another person with the intent to commit, or to aid or abet, an unlawful activity. It refers to crimes in which someone wrongfully obtains and uses another person's personal data using fraud or deception.

Although this crime has been around for years, the convenient access to personal data on Internet has made it easy for someone to perpetrate the crime with little fear of getting caught.

Unlike your DNA, fingerprints, and appearance which are unique to you and cannot be easily used by someone else, your Social Security number, bank account, credit card, or telephone calling card number can be easily exploited by others to personally profit at your expense.

In the past few years of the "Information Age", states Attorneys General and the federal government have received thousands of reports of fake checks, credit card charges, ATM withdrawals and even purchases of vehicles and expensive electronics perpetrated by unauthorized persons using other peoples identities.

The losses to the victim are not trivial. Although some protection is provided by credit card companies, losses from the use of debit cards, checks, and online bank accounts can cause complete and unlimited financial ruin—with little chance of recovery. This damage can be compounded by the legal and administrative financial costs associated with the correction of erroneous information for which the criminal was responsible.

Identity theft has another ugly dimension. It is surreptitious. When you are the victim, you have no idea of what's going on. The thief simply uses your data to buy things and then has the bills sent to a empty mail drop. It really doesn't matter where, because the thief has no intention of paying them any way. He or she just uses your data to change the billing addresses of the falsely obtained credit cards and bank statements. You normally won't find out until the damage is done and the thief is on to someone else.

Modus Operandi

Identity theft is not a recent phenomenon. Today's identity thief using your credit card to buy gas is the same guy who forged checks a few years ago. *The Internet however, has raised this old crime to a new art form.* Why? Because computers have automated the tedious tasks the criminal had to do manually in the past.

Getting your Numbers

The simple act of acquiring your credit card number, date of expiration, and issuing address is an excellent example. In the past criminals had to physically acquire this information. Criminals used to have to "shoulder surf" to get your telephone calling card credit card number—looking over your shoulder or listening to you as you gave it at a hotel desk or rental car company. Others "dumpster dived" through your trash can for checks, bank statements, and other records with your name and numbers.

All of this was time and trouble for the criminal; not to mention somewhat odiferous.

Filling out Forms

Recently however, the Internet has simplified this task by orders of magnitude. No longer does the criminal have to root through garbage to get your credit card number, he just puts up a web-site and waits for you to enter everything he needs—your credit card number, full name, address, expiration date, and even your mother's maiden name.

Guessing your Password

Requiring you to enter a password is even more clever. With all the different "services" on the Internet, most people use the same password. Don't think the thief won't try it on your online banking account.

Filling out your Profile

Identity theft is an infection: the more the thief knows about you, the more he can damage you. Once the identity thief has acquired enough information about you from the Internet, he can simply apply for a credit report on you to get the rest. If he subscribes to Equifax, TransUnion, or Experion, he needs merely to use the personal data he got from you to request a credit report.

Take a close look at your credit report someday. It's got past addresses, references, car loans, homes, phone numbers and a record of the jobs you had. This is your complete history.

In the era of electronic commerce where the parties frequently never meet, a criminal can get everything he needs to successfully transact business in your name.

Invading your Privacy—Step by step

You become more valuable to the Dotcon artist as he learns more about you. Not only can he sell your personal data for more to advertisers, but he can also use it to gain more information about you. In the world of the Dotcon artist, all information is not the same in value. Some things they know about you are more important than others.

E-mail Address

Getting your e-mail address may seem a small step for you, but it's a giant leap for them. This is normally the first piece of data in your file. When you get an e-mail address, you're on a list. People will sell that list to others, and you will start to receive e-mail. They may not know who you are yet, but they know that you exist. Now they can keep track of you.

Name

The next step is to associate your e-mail address with a name or a number. This connection turns you from an anonymous address to a real person—a real person with a credit card and a bank account.

You may underestimate the information in your e-mail address. If your address is "Ghost@aol.com", you may be safe. On the other hand, "MarkEasy@ucsd.edu" is a lot easier to profile. You're Mark Easy, a student or a professor at the University of California at San Diego.

Note the domain name. The bigger the domain and the more general your e-mail name, the more difficult it is to pick you out. "JohnS@uscd.edu" is harder to find than "JSmith@Smitty.com".

Address and Phone Number

Most e-commerce sites now ask for your address for a credit card purchase online. They use the zip code to confirm that it's you. It's good that they are. But you make it easy to be defrauded when you voluntarily enter your address and phone number for a trivial reason—to enter a "contest" or get a "free e-mail for life".

You may think that this is not particularly revealing. After all, your address and phone number are in the book. You're right in a way. *But remember all of this data is now tied to your e-mail address.* You're now worth a little more to the people who want to sell you something, get you to vote for them, or catch you doing something wrong.

So then next time you enter "sports betting " into a search engine, don't be surprised if you get a phone call from somebody who wants to sell you a tip sheet, or a visit from somebody with a badge.

Social Security Number

Your SSN is the master key to the door of your privacy. When criminals tie your Social Security Number to your name, they can now order a Credit Report from any of the three major credit reporting agencies that will reveal everything else about you and your family–birth dates, relatives, past residences, arrests, judgments, and your private financial information.

The Social Security Administration introduced the nine-digit numbers in 1935 to keep track of our earnings for tax purposes and Social Security benefits. But most companies today use the numbers for their database. When the Dotcon artist has your SSN along with your personal information, he has access to all the records associated with it.

Credit Card Number

Like your SSN is the key to your privacy, your credit card number is the latch on your purse. Credit cards have become the medium of choice when making purchases over the Internet because your personal liability is limited to $50 of the charges *after you notify the company that your card has been misused.*

But entering your credit card number on the Internet is different that giving it to a clerk at a local store. When you enter your credit card number into an insecure web-site, it travels in clear text world wide and can be theoretically picked up by any of the millions of nodes of the Internet. When you enter it into a secure web-site, it can only be decoded by the recipient.

Birth Date

A seemingly innocuous piece of data, your birth date is valuable to the Dotcon artist to confirm your identity. Like a zip code, it can be expressed as a number and is discrete. It is therefore used by banks, along with your SSN to identify you when you call. With your birth date, the Identity Thief can inquire about your bank account and perhaps have the billing address changed on your credit card.

Username

Your user-name is tied to your profile as soon as possible. These data are worth little by themselves, but in combination with your identification, they offer a window into your soul to the Internet entrepreneur, legal and illegal.

Whenever you enter a chatroom, focus group, discussion group, forum, or auction, the information you enter is associated with your username–theoretically an "anonymous" identity. When that anonymity is preserved , your bids, blasphemy and balderdash are useful to the Information mongers only as a statistic. "Twenty percent now use Tide". "Ten percent are clinically depressed." But when your username is not anonymous, then any data, bid, or comments you make are associated with you and sold to the highest bidder. *You* don't like Tide, and *you* are clinically depressed!

Passwords

Certain bits of information are more valuable to the identity thief because they act in combination with other data to provide access to important parts of your life. For instance, associating your name with an e-mail address identifies you as a likely target, and adding a SSN confirms it. Combinations of usernames and passwords open the door to your private transactions, bids, investments, and even the thoughts you express in private forums.

But certainly everybody knows passwords are secret. After all, they appear as little asterisks, so that no one can read them over your shoulder. You even forget your own password. Nobody deliberately reveals their password, do they?

Not deliberately. The problem is that you frequently use the same username and password over and over again. And the Dotcon artist expects that. If he can buy the username/password combination for your private "COOKING TIPS" account, he needs only to try it with your online bank account.

Here is a blatant attempt by a Dotcon artist pretending to be an AOL account administrator to capture your screen name and your password. AOL warned its users about this in the summer of 1999. *The "Community Action Page" was a fraud.*

> Dear <screenname>,
>
> We are sorry to inform you that we have received numerous reports of a Screen Name under this account violating the Terms Of Service [TOS].
>
> The reports have been so extensive that we must investigate this problem and therefore need you to visit our America Online Information Web Page to verify that you are in fact the REAL paying customer of this account.
>
> If you chose not to visit our *Community Action Page* or if you do and fill in incorrect information, we will have no choice but terminate your membership to America Online.

. Upon completion of our information survey and correct information is validated, we will notify you as soon as we find the person or persons that have illegally obtained your account.

Terms Of Service

Thank You,
Community Action Team

Putting it Together

Once your name and address is associated with a cookie that holds other information about you, then the database includes the user's name, address, retail, catalog and online purchase history, demographic data as well as other information collected by other Web sites and businesses.

Information mongers consider you to be a lengthy record with thousands of blanks to fill in. The form becomes more valuable as it becomes more complete. And each time you touch the keyboard or mouse there's an opportunity, however slight, to capture another tiny bit of information about you . *When more and more private data is known about millions and millions of people, the effects on privacy could be staggering.*

USERNAME1	=>MARKER
USERNAME2	=>?
USERNAME3	=>?
LASTNAME	=>EASY
FIRSTNAME	=>MARK
MI	=>?
SADDRESS	=>123 W. St
CITY	=>SAN DIEGO
STATE	=>CA
DEPRESSED	=>YES
LIKES TIDE	=>NO

```
....              =>?
....              =>?
....              =>?
....              =>?
....              =>?
....              =>?
```

Progression of Identity Theft

Personal experience, research and analysis of actual cases involving identity theft show a progressive set of similar symptoms.

The Catch

Let's say you are a hard-working, law-abiding bartender with good credit. You sign up with a free Internet provider that is advertising on TV. A little voice inside you asks why you are getting this service for free, but you go ahead and enter a screen full of personal information—your name, occupation, marital status, kids, and a host of other data that seems trivial. You feel safe because they don't ask for your Social Security Number. You hesitate occasionally to ask yourself why they want this information, but then you enter it anyway—telling yourself it's worth it because you're getting free E-mail for life.

You're not getting something for nothing. You're getting free e-mail in return for the information you are entering about yourself and your family. The Internet provider will use this, add more, and sell it again and again.

The Con

Several weeks later you get an e-mail from another bartender addressing you by your first name and suggesting you visit a new web-site that offers a Health Plan for bartenders. You click on the little blue underlined letters that say "www.bartenders-are-us.com". Your hard-disk churns and a simple web-site slowly appears with a large picture of a bartender from a

Budweiser ad and a list of blue text. You click on the one that says Health Plans. The screen clears and an official-looking advertisement appears offering you an incredible deal on health coverage. You just need to enter some information at the bottom of the page.

You fill out your name and address, phone, and then check the blocks that offer coverage for your wife, your kids, and your dog. Paging down to the bottom of the form, you then click on lists and boxes that describe your job, working conditions, health, and drinking and smoking habits.

After you've spent a half-hour entering the data, you get to the Social Security Number. You leave that one blank, and then continue to the end and press "Send". The hard-disk churns, the screen clears and a message says "Congratulations, Fred. we're processing your approval at this time." You sit back with a smile and wait.

Several minutes later the form comes back up and tells you that you left something out. You page down to see the SSN blank blinking at you, with a little message box entitled "Secure Data Encryption" next to a little picture of a lock. Understandably reluctant to enter your SSN, you feel safer when you read the message in the box, *"Please use our Secure Data Server to enter your Social Security Number."*

You enter the SSN. The hard-disk churns again, and then a another message appears next to a checked box that says, "This information may be used to obtain a credit report for family health coverage." You click "Send" again, and the final message says you'll be contacted by e-mail.

This web-site bought a list of bartenders from the ISP offering the "Free E-mail for Life", and they're getting you to enter all of your health information. They got just about everything they wanted the first time. But you were kind enough to add the Social Security Number and authorize them to get a credit report on you too.

The Apology

A week later you get an e-mail saying that your application for health benefits had been disapproved.

These guys aren't selling anything to you. They're building a database on bartenders and selling the information they find out about you to somebody else. They probably didn't run the Credit Report, but they've got your permission to do so on file if somebody wants to pay for the information.

The Hit

Two months later, you start getting calls from Amex, your two credit card companies, and Sears asking when you are going to pay last month's bill. Then your bank calls to tell you your account is overdrawn.

When you tell them this is the first you've heard of this, you are surprised to find the bills were sent a month ago and you owe a total of $18,596 dollars.

Somebody bought your Social Security Number and got a Credit Report that had your credit cards and Sears accounts on it. They changed the billing addresses to a maildrop so that you wouldn't find out.

Shortly thereafter, your credit card is confiscated by a gas station attendant who informs you that there's a fraud alert out on that number. When you call the credit card company, they ask you to recite a litany of personal data and then tell you that your card has been canceled pending "review" of your file.

Within the next few weeks, you are swamped with calls from creditors you've never heard of. They are not convinced when you tell them you are not responsible for the debt. They continue to call, and soon you find that your credit has been ruined by their reports that you are delinquent. Like a disease, the damage gets worse as the Identity theft goes undetected. Some thieves can get enough information about you to buy cars, get loans, and even commit crimes.

The person who got your SSN and data has already moved on to someone else by the time you find out what has happened.

The Myth of Secure E-Commerce

You may recall that the Internet started life as a back-up military command and control system. After thirty years of development, it has never been used for that purpose! Why?

The Internet is characteristically unsuited for secure data transmission.

"Secure" information systems are those that can not be compromised; that is, it is difficult or impossible for someone to gain access to the data in the system or to change or stop it.

One way a system is made more secure is by restricting opportunities to "tap" into the flow of data–using a dedicated wire or fiber-optic cable rather than the telephone. Another way is to encrypt the data when it is transmitted and decrypt it when it is received so that a third party cannot use it if he gains access to it. A third way is to limit the access of the data to the sender and recipient. A system is made more secure if the sender transmits the message exclusively to the recipient and the recipient does not release it.

None of the common elements of communication security are found in the everyday operation of the Internet: packets of data in clear text are sent over shared telephone lines to millions of recipients who disseminate it at will.

Both industry and government are attempting to find technical and bureaucratic solutions to this problem. If people are hesitant to pay for something online, it makes it difficult for Internet businesses to encourage spontaneous purchases of products and services. Online businesses have responded to this challenge by adopting "Privacy Standards" and "Secure Systems".

A "Secure" system means that the data you enter at your computer will be encrypted as it flows around the Internet and decrypted by the web-site at the other end. *It does not mean that the people at the other end are prohibited from revealing it–nor does it mean that it cannot be intercepted and decrypted by a "hacker" on the way from your computer to the web-site.*

Prominent web-sites now state that they have installed "Secure Systems". Pictures of little locks adorn the home pages with statements saying "Private" and "Secure". This may make you feel like the information you enter into the site isn't going to be used by anybody else. It doesn't mean that at all!

All legitimate online merchants may wish it were, but it isn't. In fact, the little "Secure E-Commerce" pictures present yet another fertile field to exploit the naiveté of the consumer.

The Dotcon is simply a blatant lie by a web-site operator that the site is secure when it isn't–either by design or negligence. They use statements like "This site uses the latest security protocols".

In today's spinning vernacular, it all depends on what the meaning of the word "is" is. Does the phrase "latest security protocols" mean the site is secure. No! Dotcon artists can put a couple lines of code into the communication software of their web-site and claim with complete honesty that their site has "the latest security protocol." Or worse yet, they can do nothing at all. You simply can't tell.

In the case of a legitimate business, this is done to alleviate your fears of dealing with a new medium. In the case of a Dotcon, its to lower your defenses so you'll enter whatever information he's after. In either case, when you see the carefully worded statement on the home page explaining that the site is secure, you feel safer. Unaware of what the term means, if in fact it means anything at all, you will believe that your personal data has been somehow protected.

Unless the web-site clearly specifies they will not release the information you provide to anyone else, they are under no obligation to keep it private. In fact, if the web-site is in the advertising or marketing business, you can be certain that most of the information they gather about you will be for sale.

Protecting Yourself from Identity Theft

You're on the Internet. You've got an e-mail account. Most likely you've already been profiled, and you're on several lists. You can be sure that a lot of people already know a lot about you. Does it matter?

Some of the biggest businesses in the Internet world say it's good. The more they know about you the better they can "serve" you. Their argument is that if they know your occupation, age, and income they can "tailor" their advertising just to you. *The real word is "target" but there's a growing reluctance to use it outside of the industry.*

The problem is that they can "serve" you even better if they know your health, your kids' ages, your insurance coverage–and perhaps even better if they know your thoughts, sexual fantasies, and everything else about your private life. If you disagree with them and would prefer to protect your privacy, these are some things you can do:

1. Never enter your Social Security Number into any online form unless you are absolutely certain that it will be used only for that purpose.
2. Get off the e-mail lists if you can. Contact the Direct Marketing Association to request that your name be placed on its "do not call," "do not mail" and "do not e-mail" lists.
3. Avoid giving out any personal data, regardless of how mundane it seems, and be extremely cautious when someone asks you to.
4. When asked for any information, respond by asking why the person needs it. Remember legitimate businesses know full well that they are required to state why they need information when they ask for it.
5. If you are asked to provide information that should already be available, ask why they have not referred to that source.
6. Check your monthly charge card and bank statements regularly and carefully. If peculiar charges appear, immediately advise the

credit card company that your credit card number may have been misused.

7. If two or more credit card bills or bank statements have not been delivered, call the company and verify your billing address. If the billing address is not yours, tell them you did not authorize the change of address and that someone may be improperly using your accounts.

If you've been victimized by an identity thief, it will take longer to repair the damage done to your credit rating and reputation than it did for the identity thief to commit the crimes. Like any other injury, the first step is to stop the bleeding. Then begin the long process of rehabilitation.

8. Call your credit card agencies immediately and advise them of the situation.
9. Call your bank and request new account numbers, ATM cards, and PIN numbers.
10. Notify your local police and file a complaint. This is likely to have no other effect other than formally documenting the offense so that you can later dispute charges.
11. Send a copy of the complaint to the FBI and each of the credit card companies.
12. Contact credit reporting agencies and request that a security alert be placed on your account.
13. Request a free copy of your credit report.
14. Review your credit report for other false accounts or information.
15. Contact the Social Security Administration Fraud Hotline.

ONLINE INVESTMENT SWINDLES

Two men were recently prosecuted in Los Angeles for buying 130,000 shares in a bankrupt company, and then posting false messages on hundreds of Internet bulletin boards, falsely stating that it was going to be taken over by a wireless telecommunications company. The stock increased by 1000% in one morning of trading.

The Internet allows individuals to reach a large audience without spending much money. A single message can be spread to millions of investors with the click of a button. Individual Dotcon artists who own stock, or "investment services" can reach millions of users in their homes and offices by coding an Internet web-site, posting a message on an online bulletin board, entering a chatroom, or sending mass e-mails.

The Securities Exchange Commission has identified two ways that Dotcon artists manipulate securities for personal profit. They both involve volatile small capitalization stocks that can be radically influenced by information spread on a massive scale.

In the first scheme, the Dotcon artists buy the stock, disseminate false and fraudulent information and cause the price to go up—at which time they quickly sell the stock and take their profits.

In the second scheme, they sell the stock short, spread bad news to cause panic selling and then purchase the stock back as it plummets.

Pump And Dump—Going Up

In 1999, a California man was prosecuted for replicating a reputable stock information web-site, and then posting false recommendations about a company he owned stock in. The stock soared 30% before the deception was identified.

The speed of the Internet combined with the recent phenomenon of "day trading" has provided a unique opportunity for Dotcon artists to exploit the gullible. Millions of e-mails reach millions of eyeballs. And millions of fingers click "buy" before the scam can be identified. This scheme called "Pump and Dump" by the SEC combines dramatic price increases in thinly traded stocks or stocks of shell companies (the "pump"), and then quick sale (the "dump") to take profits. This scheme is not new, but the speed and stealth with which it can be accomplished is stunning.

The Investment News E-mail has replaced the unexpected telephone call telling you to buy a stock quickly or to sell before the price goes down. Like the broker on the phone five years ago, an E-mail message arrives today with the subject "URGENT". It will claim to have "inside" information about an impending development that will affect the fundamental worth of a company—either good or bad. You can be sure that the sender of the message has something to gain by influencing you.

In the "Pump and Dump" scheme they are Dotcon artists who will profit handsomely by selling their shares after the stock price is pumped up by gullible investors. When the Dotcon artists sell their shares and stop sending out the messages, the price falls and you lose your money if you don't get out quickly.

Cash and Trash—Going Down

In a recent federal prosecution described by the SEC, a day-trader repeatedly posted a false press release falsely stating that a major

telecommunications company would not meet its quarterly earn-
ings estimates. The false report drove the stock's price down and
reduced the market value of the stock by more than $7 billion.

The second scheme takes a similar approach—disseminating false or fraudulent information in an effort to cause price *decreases* in a particular company's stock. The scam is simple, and dreadfully powerful. The SEC calls it "scalping". "Cash and Trash" more accurately describes it.

It's based on the notion that people react more desperately to prevent a loss (a stock they own quickly plummeting) than they will to seize a potential gain (a new stock appreciating). The Dotcon artist:

1. Selects a small-cap, thinly traded Internet stock that has been substantially inflated since its Initial Public Offering.

2. Buys a mailing list of investors in small capitalization stocks, or uses a "Mining" program to capture e-mail names from various sources on the Internet. If he's really clever, he might even be able to buy a list of the *actual owners* of the stock in question–a Dotcon artist's bonanza.

3. Creates an e-mail message that alerts the investment community of a potential disaster about to occur to the stock he has identified. It helps if there is some substance to the rumor.

4. Logs onto his online day trading account under another identity and sells the stock short.

5. Mass mails the e-mail using an anonymous e-mail address.

6. Watches the stock go down as the online traders react to the "news".

7. Covers the short when the stock goes down 15 minutes later.

Is it naïve to believe that this simple scheme works? Ask yourself what you would do if you got an e-mail message saying that the CEO of your volatile small-cap stock is about to be indicted for fraud. Would you log-on to your trading account to check it? If it went down a couple of ticks, would you hold on to it?

Investment Newsletters

The Security Exchange Commission recently sued an Internet advertising firm that distributed an online newsletter to promote two small, thinly traded "microcap" companies. They failed to tell investors that the companies they were touting had agreed to pay them in cash and securities.

Search for "Investment Newsletter". You'll find dozens. Most of which are free. You might ask yourself why. With traditional stock information services charging thousands of dollars for confidential information that they diligently dig out, why are these companies offering you seemingly unbiased information free of charge? What are they getting out of it?

The answer is they are either getting paid to promote the stock, or they themselves own it. In either case, it is unlikely that the information you will get from a free investment newsletter is unbiased.

The intimacy and interactive nature of the Internet is a seductive means to influence even the most sophisticated investor. Rather than a bland announcement in the newspaper according to SEC regulations, you learn about Internet stocks with bright, animated, technologically enhanced web-sites designed by Dotcon artists.

Ask a question about a new technology. You'll get back a host of online newsletters "touting" several hot new issues that they have just "discovered".

Touting and Disclosure

The SEC requires newsletters to disclose who paid them, the amount, and the type of payment. But unlike conventional newsletters that are read from beginning to end, the Internet provides Dotcon artists a unique opportunity to *bury the disclosure statement so deep in the web-site that it is unlikely to be found by the investor.*

The urgency of the investment decision compounds the problem—feigned or not. "Day-traders" who profit in moments cannot spend the time to peruse the recommendation to find the hidden agenda. They read and click. Most of the time they are right.

Touting is not against the law. If it were, the prisons would be filled with advertising executives. The federal government can not stop organizations or individuals from publishing newsletters or making comments recommending particular stocks. But when these individuals or companies are paid to do it, then the law requires them to disclose it.

Legitimate web-sites know exactly what the SEC requires them to say, and they know precisely how they have to say it. Web-sites who don't disclose this, or who waffle around it, are suspect. Consider the following:

> *"On occasion, officers, directors, or staff of this service may hold stock in some of the companies we write about."*

That doesn't meet the criteria. They've got to tell you what stock they own, who owns it and how much. The SEC monitors investment sites and lists the ones that are suspect on their web-site. If you believe in a newsletter and are ready to make an investment in the stock, why not check to see if the SEC has taken any action against them before you do?

Bulletin Boards and Chatrooms

> *The SEC recently sued thirteen people who worked together to drive up the price of a stock they owned with false statements on a bulletin board claiming non-existent multi-million dollar sales and false revenue projections.*

Online bulletin boards and chatrooms have proven to be an uniquely effective means for Dotcon artists to influence your opinion. Dotcon artists pretend to reveal "inside" information about upcoming announcements, new products, or lucrative contracts on bulletin boards for the sole purpose of affecting the price of the stock.

Of course this opportunity exists in traditional media as well, but the Internet has turned it into an art-form for the Dotcon artist. People claiming to be unbiased observers who've carefully researched the company may actually be stockholders, brokers, or promoters.

Multiple Identities

In fact one person can be many. A single eager computer-savvy investor can easily stimulate buying of a small, thinly-traded stock by posting a series of messages as different people to start a conversation about a stock that he or she owns.

This clever scheme requires only that the Dotcon artist register in the chat room with several different identities–each operating in a separate window. Signing on as "MBA", he touts the management expertise of the company, as "CodeMonkey" he complains about how difficult it is to "hack" into the software produced by the company, as "BuyLow" he says it's never going to be a better buy, and as "Fred" he logs off to buy it.

And then it's your turn. Would you be influenced?

Protecting against Online Investment Swindles

Like any other Dotcon, your first defense against the bulletin board "pump and dump" and "cash and trash" is to recognize them for what they are–orchestrated attempts to entice you to take a position in a stock–immediately!

The urgency is the key to recognition. Remember, the little conspiracy is happening right then. If you leave the site without having made a decision to buy or the stock, then the Dotcon artist has lost his opportunity. Time then is of the essence. If you feel that you have make an investment right then and there, you're probably wrong.

Legitimate stock brokers don't need to pressure you into investing. Even "day-traders" carefully research the stocks they want to take a position in well before the time comes to do it. You should too.

Fast, accurate, timely information is an important key to investment success, and the Internet offers a wealth of legitimate information with a timeliness never before possible. If you want to exploit the benefits of this dynamic medium in the era of the Dotcon artist, you should be aware that some of this information may be exaggerated–either by conceit or deceit. Both are easy to miss if you yourself are unfamiliar with the technology.

BUSINESS VENTURE DOTCONS

In late 1999, four individuals were criminally charged in California for sending out 50 million e-mails that falsely advertised work-at-home opportunities, but provided few actual opportunities for people who paid the $35 advance fee.

These schemes use the Internet to advertise business ventures that purport to provide individuals with the opportunity to a living wage by becoming a "distributor", starting a "home-business", or purchasing a "franchise". They typically require the individuals to pay an advance fee for software, tool kits, materials or information they need to get started.

The Federal Trade Commission and a group of twenty-five State Attorneys General have begun a massive investigation of this new form of crime they have euphemistically termed 'information-highway' robbery. During the investigation they found 500 web-sites that appeared to be illegal pyramid schemes, and estimated that these kind of scams succeed with millions of people and cost Internet users over $350 million a year.

Business Venture Dotcons are characterized by banners on web-sites and phrases on the subject line of e-mails such as: "Start your own Web business," "Cash in on the Internet", "Make millions on your home computer", "Double your money every month", and "Turn $5 into $60,000 in just three to six weeks." Do these phrases look familiar? They should.

They're the same headlines that you got in the mail five years ago. They've just been adapted to fit the latest venue by the Dotcon artist.

The swindle is that the ads do not accurately represent the amount of work you must do, the money you will make, the money you will have to spend up front, or the people who have succeeded in the venture.

They don't say that you may have to work many hours without pay, or there are hefty costs on your end. Countless work-at-home schemes require you to spend your own money to buy computer software, email lists, and other supplies or equipment you need to do the job. The websites sponsoring the ads also may demand that you pay for instructions or materials. Consumers deceived by these ads have lost thousands of dollars in start-up costs and wasted months of time and energy.

The Ponzi

On March 22, 2000, four people were indicted in Cleveland for committing mail wire fraud for carrying out a "Ponzi" scheme on the Internet that collected more than $26 million from "investors" without selling any product or service. They paid older investors with the proceeds of the money collected from the newer investors

Ponzi schemes are investment frauds that have been around since the 1920's—the first one perpetrated by a Mr. Charles Ponzi. The Ponzi scheme looks like a conventional investment opportunity—an oil well, gold mine or real estate. The promoter may own it, or it may not exist, but he claims to needs money from investors to develop it. He convinces investors that the asset can be further developed with more capital, and he promises to share the profits with the investors.

He collects investments from the investors, and then announces that the venture has been successful–paying impressive early dividends and telling them that they are "shared profits" coming from the well or mine. In fact he's merely returning a portion of the investors money to them.

The large early dividends encourage the existing investors to invest more and attract others to the scheme. The con artist does this until he can't pay a dividend and then vanishes with the rest of the money.

Mr. Ponzi would have loved the Internet. He could only reach a dozen or so friends to start the thing. Dotcon artists can reach a few million at once with the click of a mouse. One of them might be you!

The Pyramid

A Pyramid scheme is a plan similar to the Ponzi wherein you pay for the opportunity to receive compensation that is derived primarily from that your introduction of other people to participate in the plan.

Pyramid schemes are illegal in most states because the plans inevitably collapse when no new distributors can be recruited. When a plan collapses, most people, except those at the top of the pyramid, lose their money.

It differs from a "Multi-Level-Marketing" business in that an MLM is supposed to produce income from the sale of products rather than the introduction of new people. The difference is crucial. You can go to jail for a pyramid scheme–it's a felony! This difference appears to have escaped most of the Dotcon artists.

The logic by which a Pyramid unfolds is indeed the magic of using the Internet to do it. One person gets ten people to pay ten dollars to start the plan. Each of the ten get ten more, keep half of the ten dollars and pass the remainder up. Each of those get ten, each of those get ten, and each of those get ten, ad infinitum.

Fourth grade math will tell you that the seventh guy down the chain is in a group of ten million people (10 to the 7th), and is really going to have to hustle to find someone in the neighborhood who hasn't already joined the crowd or passed on the opportunity.

The Dotcon artists try to beat the system by subtly introducing a product or service into the Pyramid, thereby making it appear to be a legal Multi-Level-Marketing system. One such scheme prosecuted in Texas purported to be a network of "E-mail Processing Agents" whose job is to send e-mails to recruit other "Agents" into the program who in turn will send e-mails to recruit others. The product is an "E-mail Processing Kit" that ends up to be a trivial computer program that keeps track of the recruitment of new "Agents" who buy the kit for $50 and sell it to more "Agents". The scheme was judged to be illegal because the E-mail Processing Kit wasn't worth $50. The primary source of revenue was the recruitment of new agents.

Work at Home Frauds

The "Work at Home" fraud is an apparently legal business opportunity where the Dotcon artist develops a sophisticated web-site and uses fake predictions of profitability and other misrepresentations to lure investors into believing they can make thousands of dollars a month working at home. There are usually lots of testimonials.

Traditional schemes involve the purchase of parts and tools to put something together that could be sold, fabric and designs to make clothes, or sales opportunities addressing letters, stuffing envelopes and mass mailing solicitations to thousands of other people with the same or similar offer.

Many of the Dotcons are merely electronic variations of these old themes, but in this case you're buying parts to put computers together, or software to create web-sites, make greeting cards, do taxes, bill clients, collect debts, or send mass e-mails.

The allure of the offer is far more appealing today. After all, think of the time and effort it would take to address and stuff a thousand envelopes. Now you can do a hundred thousand e-mails with the click of a mouse. And you don't have to buy any expensive machinery. You've already got a computer. You just have to buy the software. And you'll make your investment back in the first mailing. So it says right here.

You will find it hard to find anything wrong with the work-at-home programs advertised on the Internet. The Dotcon artist rightly claims that you can e-mail two million people in less than a day with his software and mailing list. And you only need a 1% response rate to become a millionaire by the end of the year.

The deceit is in the response rate. The 1% is wrong. People don't respond to junk mail. Stuffing envelopes didn't work before, and Spam doesn't work today for the same reason. Your e-mail gets lost in the vast wasteland of junk e-mail that is being generated every day. Compound this with the proliferation of Dotcon scams, and you can be sure that the people who do read your e-mail are not eager buyers. They are skeptical of any unsolicited offer. You should be too!

E-mail Re-mail

Some promoters advertise that they will tell you how to earn money using your computer at home–for a small fee. After you've paid the fee, you get an HTML document attached to an e-mail explaining how to send the same e-mail *that you bit off on* to other suckers.

The Dotcon artist might also deliver instructions to download a program that will allow you to generate your own mailing lists.

Computer Work

These programs require you to invest money up-front to buy computer parts, software, supplies, and training. Your job is to assemble a computer or develop a program that the web-site will buy from you. For example, you might buy computer parts and assemble a computer, or software to create a web-site, a graphics program to make signs and logos, or a program to generate mailing lists.

This business venture is appealing to you, because it looks straight— you make money on honest labor. The Dotcon is that the company that you bought the parts and supplies from has no intention of paying you for the final product.

They get away with it by claiming that your work didn't meet "quality standards." Unfortunately, no work is ever up to standards.

Recognizing the Dotcon

Certainly not all business opportunities on the Internet are fraudulent, and working at home is becoming more popular every day. How can you determine whether or not the offer is legitimate? It's possible that the hook of the Dotcon is hidden somewhere in the fine print–or buried three clicks deep in the architecture of the web-site. In cases like this, It's a good idea to have a specific response to the following questions. E-mail these to the offered. If its a Dotcon, he won't respond.

- What are the phone numbers of the testimonials?
- What exactly must I do?
- How much do I get paid to do it?
- Who pays me?
- When do I get paid?
- Will I be paid by cash, check or credit card?
- How much do I have to pay you to do this?
- What do I have to buy or lease?
- When do I pay you?
- Do I have do buy anything else?
- Do I have do anything else?
- How do I get my money back?

The New Concept Investment

Last year, The SEC stopped a web-site from soliciting investors for a proposed eel farm over the Internet. The offer promised investors a "whopping 20% return," claiming that the investment was "low risk."

This Dotcon is a legitimate business opportunity that requires an advance payment on the part of the investor and includes a statement that there is a low risk that the investor will lose the money he put up front. It is characterized by a new technology or breakthrough and varies from investments in wireless cable projects to prime bank securities, cures for diseases, Internet "infrastructure" products, laser research, and even eel farms.

Few new concepts or technologies are free of risk, and purporting otherwise should alert you to the fact that there is something amiss. "Large returns" simply do not coexist with "Low Risk" investments. A high rate of return means greater risk.

Even worse than high risk investments, the SEC has found sophisticated web-sites touting investment products that did not even exist. Dotcons operating from off-shore locations are particularly well-suited for this brazen scam. When you send your money abroad and something goes wrong, there are no federal agencies that can get it back.

Training and Orientation Seminars

Everyone who starts a new business needs training, or at least thinks so. Legitimate businesses hire you first and then train you on their time. Macdonald's includes training with the cost of the franchise. In normal circumstances, training is part of the package. If it's not, why not?

It's because the Dotcon artist is using an orientation course to sell you something else in person. This Dotcon is especially effective in Internet start-up scams. The Internet can do lots of things well. One thing it can't do is replace a hand-shake, a smile, and a persuasive salesperson to sell you a high value item like an Internet Start-up Business.

A web-site may give you all the data you need to believe that you can earn thousands of dollars a week at home by starting an Internet company, but it will rarely convince you to fork over thousands of dollars on your debit card. The Dotcon artist does that by getting you into a conference room with other "enthusiastic" participants.

The idea is to hook you with the Internet and sell you intellectually–then get you into a "free" seminar where you can be sold emotionally.

These meetings are carefully scripted. You'll be surprised that the people from the company know everything about you. Remember when you filled out the "qualification sheet" on the web-site at "no cost or obligation". You listed your current job, experience, marital status, and probably your income. *Hmmm....*

When you arrive, you will be greeted by your first name and psychologically manipulated to write out a check for a several thousand dollars–being assured that this is a small investment that will lead to a new million-dollar business.

There are many fascinating opportunities on the Internet. If you find yourself sitting in a free seminar with a dozen other people listening to a computer whiz talk about making millions of dollars, this is probably not one of them.

Federal Job Dotcons

This Dotcon promotes "hidden job opportunities with the Federal Government". They offer to help you locate and apply for Federal jobs for a fee. Some companies represent themselves with names that imply affiliation with the Federal Government, such as the "Federal Employment Agency," or "Postal Employment Service."

The deceptive element of this Dotcon is that these companies advertise large numbers of Federal jobs in local areas that don't exist. When you apply for them, they are filled.

You can find information on job vacancies with the Federal Government free of charge on the Internet by visiting their sites. The U.S.

Office of Personnel Management's Federal Employment Information System is the official source for employment information and contains Federal job listings as well as some state, local government and private sector listings.

Disclosure

It is foolish to suggest that you should not invest in new business opportunities or technologies just because they appear on the Internet. How to invest is the question. How can you tell whether or not the company's statements are correct?

Some business opportunities found on the Internet appear to be pyramid schemes, but legally are not. Rather they may be legitimate Multi-level Marketing operations—legal ways of selling goods and services through distributors. Some others claim scores of satisfied "distributors" or "franchisers". How can you tell the difference between a legitimate business and an illegal marketing scheme?

The FTC requires that businesses of this kind comply with the *Franchise Rule*. That means they must disclose the number and percentage of existing franchisees who have achieved the claimed results. If you're interested in a Business Opportunity, but it looks like a scheme, then just e-mail the seller and ask them to send you a signed disclosure sheet in accordance with the FTC Franchise Rule. It should tell you how many other people have done it, and how much they are making. If you don't hear back from them, they were a Dotcon. If you get the disclosure, the FTC *Rule* requires franchise and business opportunity sellers to give you at least 10 days to review it before you pay any money or commit to a purchase.

According to the FTC, the document must include:
• names, addresses, and telephone numbers of other purchasers;
• a fully-audited financial statement of the seller;

- the background and experience of the business's key executives;
- the cost of starting and maintaining the business; and the responsibilities of the seller and purchaser once the purchase is made
- the number and percentage of owners who have done at least as well as claimed.
- earnings representations that provide a written basis for their claims.

Protecting Against Business Venture Dotcons

The big difference between Business Venture scams perpetrated by mail and e-mail is that the Post Office can physically stop a mail order scam by enforcing the postal laws, confiscating the mailing piece, or sending a Postal Inspector to the source. When they deceive with a brochure, it's postal fraud. When they use an e-mail or web-site, it's up to you to protect yourself.

- Evaluate the business opportunity not the web-site. Dotcon artists create classy web-sites in a few days, operate a scam, and then shut down in a week in almost complete anonymity.
- Evaluate the facts not the allegations. Read the disclosure document not the testimonials.
- Do not invest until you have contacted several other owners or franchisees listed in the disclosure document
- Check the actual profits of the other franchisees or owners. These must be in the disclosure document.
- Take at least ten days before you sign anything—or give anybody any money. The FTC rule was made for your benefit—not the sellers.
- Get the sales contract in writing—and signed. The transitory nature of e-mails makes them less enforceable than a hard copy of a contract signed by both parties on a specific date.
- Have an accountant look over the finances and promised income.
- Avoid plans that pay commissions for recruiting others.

- Beware of plans that require you to purchase inventory up front.
- Be cautious of schemes that claim you do little or no work.
- Insist on proof that the product works. Check with an independent source to make sure that you aren't being deceived.
- Beware of shills—people paid by the web-site for testimonials in the disclosure document.
- Don't agree to anything in a high pressure meeting or seminar. Insist on having time to think it over.
- Get a complete description of the work involved before you send any money.
- Don't pay for a job description.
- Don't pay to attend a training seminar before you invest.
- Be suspicious of requests for up-front fees. Most legitimate agencies only charge if they actually produce.
- Don't believe promises of access to a "hidden job market."
- Be skeptical of any employment service firm that guarantees refunds if you meet certain criteria. You probably don't qualify.
- Get a copy of the firm's contract and review it carefully before paying.
- Be aware that some listing services and "consultants" may place ads that seem to offer jobs when in fact they are selling resume services up front.
- Get the refund, buy-back and cancellation policies in writing.
- Take the contract to your lawyer.

ADVANCE FEE SCAMS

"Car loans. Bad Credit. No Credit, OK!", "Home Loans–Nothing down!" "Business Start-up Capital", "Get Venture Capital!"

This is a quintessential confidence game that is ideal for the Internet. It involves paying in advance for a product or service that is not delivered. It works because you have "confidence" that the perpetrator is honest. This used to be hard for the con artist because he had to "convince" you in person or by phone. Most people weren't stupid enough to send cash in the mail to an anonymous vendor. The Internet changed all that. Most people are.

The Dotcon artist can now do all of it electronically–develop confidence with a prestigious web-site, answer your questions automatically, and then take your credit card order.

Modus Operandi

In the typical Advance Fee Dotcon, the web-site tricks you into paying in advance to perform a service that is difficult for you to do yourself–get a car loan, a credit card, or a home loan, repair your credit, or find investors for your business. The site convinces you that they can do this better than you can by electronically "shopping" your credentials to hundreds of private sources.

As you browse the web-site, you find glowing praise and testimonials from the dozens of satisfied customers who thank the Dotcon artist for saving them from financial ruin, or making it possible for them to get the house they've always wanted.

You pay the advance fee, but unfortunately the loan, credit card, or other service you expected is never awarded. Sadly you are advised by e-mail that your application was turned down by all of the sources.

The Dotcon is classic. You have "confidence" that the Dotcon artist can do the job, so you pay him in advance. The only illegal part of it is that he Dotcon artist misrepresents the facts that he can actually do this if you've not been able to. The fact is that his process of sending your application to credit card agencies will be no more successful than you were. If you've been turned down by one or two in the past, so will he.

Agency Dotcons

This Advance fee Dotcon preys on frustrated inventors, computer programmers and authors—creative people who have spent hundreds of hours creating something and then can't sell it or market it. The web-site or e-mail promises to "represent" your invention, book, or computer program if it meets their business criteria.

You describe your creation and are elated when you receive an e-mail back telling you of the fortunes that will be made. They offer to evaluate your product, book, or program and provide a plan of action for a small fee. You pay the fee, and receive a glowing proposal to market your creation to thousands of firms for another fee of only $795.

Since you already paid them a small fee, you now have "confidence" that they are a legitimate firm. You pay them up-front.

You get back an e-mail every month for about six months before they regretfully inform you that no one was interested in your product, book, or program. Nobody returns your voice-mail messages.

The Nigerian Advance Fee Scam

In June of 1995, an American was murdered in Lagos, Nigeria,
while pursuing the following scam.

The Nigerian Advance Fee Scam has been around for at least fifteen years, but despite many warnings, it is still being spread on the Internet.

The goal of the Dotcon artist is to convince the person who receives the e-mail into thinking that he or she has been specially selected for a "secret" financial arrangement Upon receipt of a positive response, the victim is sent sealed documents under official Nigerian government letterhead, along with false credit references and bank drafts.

The references themselves are e-mail addresses that the Dotcon artist has carefully established for himself or trusted agents. When the victim is satisfied that the proposal is legitimate he is introduced to a "high Nigerian official" in a secret meeting.

When the victim is ready to close the deal, the Dotcon artist then announces a snag in the process—a tax must be paid. The multi-million dollar deal will fall through unless the victim can help pay the tax to the Nigerian government will have to be paid before the money can be transferred.

Shortly after the fee is paid, another is required, and then another, but each time the fee is described as the last fee required. The process continues until the mark runs out of money or calls the authorities—the Secret Service.

Lagos, Nigeria.
Attention: The President/CEO
Dear Sir,
Confidential Business Proposal
Having consulted with my colleagues and based on the information gathered from the Nigerian Chambers Of Commerce And

Industry, I have the privilege to request for your assistance to transfer the sum of $47,500,000.00 (forty seven million, five hundred thousand United States dollars) into your accounts. The above sum resulted from an over-invoiced contract, executed commissioned and paid for about five years (5) ago by a foreign contractor. This action was however intentional and since then the fund has been in a suspense account at The Central Bank Of Nigeria Apex Bank.

We are now ready to transfer the fund overseas and that is where you come in. It is important to inform you that as civil servants, we are forbidden to operate a foreign account; that is why we require your assistance. The total sum will be shared as follows: 70% for us, 25% for you and 5% for local and international expenses incident to the transfer.

The transfer is risk free on both sides. I am an accountant with the Nigerian National Petroleum Corporation (NNPC). If you find this proposal acceptable, we shall require the following documents:

(a) your banker's name, telephone, account and fax numbers.

(b) your private telephone and fax numbers.

(c) your letter-headed paper stamped and signed.

Alternatively we will furnish you with the text of what to type into your letter-headed paper, along with a breakdown explaining, comprehensively what we require of you. The business will take us thirty (30) working days to accomplish.

It seems astounding that the scam still works, but it does. Primarily because it depends upon your keeping the "secret" and continuing to protect your investment with relatively small contributions of cash in comparison to the enormous promised payoff.

According to the how deep you fall into the plot, you may be requested to make even greater commitments; for example, it is not uncommon for victims to travel to Nigeria to pay-off the bribe. Once there, the con artist uses accomplices to coerce the victims into releasing funds.

The Financial Crimes Division of the Secret Service handles hundreds of reports like this every day.

Defenses against Advance Fee Scams

Like other Dotcons, the best defense against the Advance Fee Scam is to recognize it for what it is—an attempt to get you to pay in advance for services that will be rendered. The first thing you should ask is why you have to pay in advance. Are you asked to pay your lawyer, dentist, plumber, or TV repairman in advance? That's just not the way most legitimate businesses operate. Legitimate credit card issuers don't ask for money up front unless you're applying for a secured card. If you are, make sure you understand how your deposit will be used.

If this web-site is to deliver a service to you, why does it require you to pay in advance? You may surmise that it's because the business providing the service distrusts the consumer. Ask yourself if you really want to do business with a faceless business that doesn't trust *you*?

Avoid paying advance fees for anything. Shop around for services and offer to pay when the service has been successfully completed. Most legitimate vendors who want your business may offer the same service on a contingency basis and bill you later. Try to pay for products after they're delivered and you've had a chance to be sure you got what you ordered.

If the web-site states you must pay in advance, try e-mailing the business first and telling them that you will pay them after the product or service is delivered. If they intend to deliver on their promise, they may agree. If not, insist on a written guarantee, and read it carefully. It may say something entirely different from the flashy announcement on the home page. *If the guarantee is not on the web-site and they won't e-mail it to you, you're dealing with a Dotcon.*

CREDIT FRAUD ON THE INTERNET

In September of 1999 the FTC filed complaints against two Arizona-based companies for selling "services" that protected against credit-card fraud, after making unauthorized charges to consumers' credit-card accounts using their credit card numbers.

Credit cards have become the default medium of exchange on the Internet, because credit-card companies limit the liability of the consumer if his or her card is stolen and used to charge purchases.

There are two common ways to defraud you on the Internet. If you've got good credit, Dotcon artists get your credit card number and use it to make purchases. If you've got bad credit, they try to convince you to pay money up front for them to "repair" it.

Credit Card Number Fraud

The Dotcon artist executing this scam sets up a web-site or an e-mail solicitation in which users make small purchases online with their credit cards. He delivers the product as advertised, but he either sells the number and data to somebody else or uses it to charge items online with an anonymous e-mail name and address. If and when the victims get billed for the purchases, the web-site has already been shut down by its anonymous owner.

The key to this Dotcon is to get you to enter your name, address, credit card number and expiration date. The combination of your name, number and the zip code from your address are lethal. With this information, a criminal can use your credit card to charge products on the Internet, have them shipped to an anonymous maildrop, and change your billing address so that you won't find out about it for months.

Your first indication is likely to be a telephone call from your credit card company asking when you are going to pay last month's bill. When you tell them you have not received it, you are surprised to find it was a month ago and it was a couple thousand dollars more than you remember charging.

After a short discussion, you tell them your card must have been stolen–and they tell you that you are only responsible for $50 of the charges *after this notification.*

What about the thousands of dollars of charges before the phone call? They are in "dispute." Your credit card is not renewed, and soon you find that your credit record has been annotated to that effect.

Credit Card Protection Plans

All credit card protection plans are Dotcons.

They are trying to exploit your ignorance of the law should your credit card be lost or stolen. Under federal law, $50 is the maximum you would legally owe on bogus charges under these circumstances. Whether or not the charge is bogus or not is partially determined by when you reported it stolen; however, in any case, the law allows you not to pay while charges are in "dispute".

The Dotcon is that the fine print of the protection scheme merely offers to report the misuse of your card if you haven't and then reiterates the guarantee of the Federal law–no more no less.

If the dispute doesn't work out in your favor with the credit card company, the credit card protection plan will not cover it either.

Third-Party Credit Card Scams

A Dotcon artist with *somebody else's* credit card number can also use that number to victimize *you!* He sets up a web-site that sells name-brand items on the Internet at bargain prices that are less than any legitimate e-commerce competitor–and invites comparisons. *When you contact the web-site to buy the item, he lowers your defenses by promising to ship it before you have to pay for it.*

Believing the web-site to be legitimate because you didn't have to provide your credit card number, you agree to purchase it. The Dotcon artist then uses your name and address along with the unlawfully obtained credit card number belonging to somebody else to buy the item at a legitimate web-site.

You get the item as advertised, and then happily authorize your credit card to be billed by the Dotcon artist. Confusing, but this is what happened:

1. You got a bargain.
2. The Dotcon artist got your money.
3. The person who owns the credit card number got billed.
4. The legitimate merchant got stiffed.
5. The process took several months to figure out.
6. The Dotcon artist is long gone.

Online Credit Reports

This is a subtle way of grossly invading your privacy without your knowledge. Third parties get your permission to obtain your credit report from the legitimate Credit Reporting Agencies every month and put it "online" so that you can review it. This "service" costs you about $70 annually. You get to see the "private" information that is being published about you–and the third party legally gets to put it all in their database for sale to anybody who wants it. This is a massive invasion of privacy that leaves you vulnerable to all kinds of problems in the future.

Restrictions on Credit Reporting Agencies

There are three major credit reporting agencies that sell information about you to businesses every time you apply for a loan, a rental, a mortgage, an account, or other agreement involving credit. These reports contain detailed information about your life and your family–not only all your financial data, but also your social-security number, drivers licenses, past residences, jobs, references, employers, law suits, court records, and anything other information about you that they choose to retain and publish. *Nothing is off limits.*

With the advent of the computer age, the collection and dissemination of this data became such a violation of privacy that Congress passed the Fair Credit Reporting Act to prohibit Credit Reporting Agencies from revealing your personal data to third-parties without your permission. This act covers the release of this data on the Internet as well–but only by the Credit Reporting Agencies themselves.

Online Websites

Third parties who legally obtain this information from the Credit Reporting Agencies can use it any way they want to! When you apply for an "Online Credit Report", you are giving them this permission–indefinitely–unless you tell them to stop.

The Online Credit Report websites simply get your report from a legitimat Credit Reporting Agency every month like you would, put all the information in a database, and generate a webpage for you to see when you visit their site. Seems harmless until you realize that they are selling that information to anybody who wants it–Scam artists, the IRS, Creditors, Lawyers, and law enforcement agencies all over the country.

The deception is slight, subtle, and arguably perfectly legal. You click on a banner that might have the name of a major Credit Reporting Agency in small print offering a "Free Online Credit Report". The screen clears and a very professional website appears telling you that there is "No need to wait for a report in the mail, when you can get it online". You don't want to wait for a report in the mail, so you complete the complex form, give them your credit card number, social security number and then press "Enter" only to find that they have to "contact you by mail" to "protect" you.

The catch to the "free" offer is you must purchase a "monitoring service," where they automatically bill the credit card number you give them again and again every month until you cancel. Some also promote 30 free days of the service, but in fact they do it every 90 days.

This would be considered a legitimate service but for the deception. You expect the "Online Credit Report" to be "online" after you enter the information and give them your credit card number. That is why you gave them your credit card. But when screen clears, it's not. Instead you are notified that you will be receiving a "passcode," in the mail to "protect" you–a hoax which gives them time to request your credit report from a Credit Reporting Agency just like you would, and type it into their database.

It takes longer to arrive in the mail than the free report from one of the actual Credit Reporting Agencies–legitimate business who are prohibited by law from revealing it without your permission.

Credit Repair Scams

All services offering to repair your credit rating for an advanced fee are scams.

It's against the law for a web-site offering credit repair to require payment before the promised services have actually been performed. This is simply an administrative matter. You're not asked to pay your accountant or lawyer in advance. If the web-site is offering to provide a service for you, why should you pay them in advance?

Call them and ask to specify exactly what they will do for you, and ask to pay for it after its done. In the case of credit repair, there is no logical reason for the offering agency not to let you pay after the service has been completed. After all, if they succeed in cleaning up your record and you don't pay them, they can simply ruin it again with a bad credit entry.

If it sounds too good to be true when you call them, ask them if you can record the phone call. If they're in another state, the Federal Telemarketing Sales Rule says they cannot even ask for payment until they've shown you proof of the promised results with a copy of your credit report that has been issued by a credit bureau more than six months after the corrections were made.

Except for licensed attorneys, a credit repair scheme can't do anything more than you can do yourself. Lawyers have a little more clout. They can effectively threaten to sue the Credit Reporting company if you have a legitimate correction that the Credit Reporting company won't change.

If there is a mistake in your credit record, contact the major credit reporting agencies and ask how to correct it. There is no fee.

If the bad credit report is accurate, then you are being deceived by the Dotcon if they say they can remove negative information–regardless of the procedure they plan to execute. Only incorrect information can be erased from your credit report. Everything else remains a part of your record for seven years from the time it is reported, except for bankruptcies that stay on your record for ten years.

The Dotcon may claim that they can enter positive information in your record that will offset the effect of the negative information so that you can restore your credit. So can you. You can include a short statement in your credit file explaining illnesses or unemployment that made it impossible for you to keep up your payments.

Another Dotcon promises to give you a "fresh start" with a new credit file. He proposes to substitute an Employer ID number for your social security number. This process is fraudulent itself. If you sign a contract for somebody else to do it, you could be subject to serious penalties.

Impact of Credit Fraud

You are affected in several ways by Credit Fraud on the Internet: you can lose money, your credit cards can be canceled, your credit can be damaged, and your privacy can be invaded as you endeavor to repair it.

You should be justifiably wary about entering your credit card numbers into a form on the Internet, but compared to other alternatives—electronic bank drafts and debit cards—it seems the lesser of two evils. Nevertheless there is a very real chance that your number can be associated with your name, expiration date, and zip code so that it can be reused by a criminal.

When this happens, your credit suffers while you struggle to fix it, and you ripen for yet another scam on the Internet—Credit Repair. You'll be contacted by e-mail by other Dotcons offering to repair the damage. You pay them in advance only to find that they cannot remove the negative information from your file. Only you can do that.

You need a copy of your credit report to start, so you sign on to the Internet and find "Online Credit Reports" yet another Dotcon where you release your credit-card number, social-security number and a host of personal data only to find that you could have gotten the information free, and you're going to have to wait for it anyway. Welcome to the Information Age!

ONLINE AUCTION FRAUDS

In 1999 the first recorded conviction for Internet auction fraud was in West Palm Beach, Fla. In a sophisticated buy-sell scheme based upon false bids on the Internet, the man falsely advertised on Internet auction sites computer components that he purported to have for sale, but did not own.

Online auctions are a popular new e-commerce business on the Internet. The world-wide scope of the Internet offers an unique opportunity for buyers and sellers to trade items that are of value to both. But because online auctions are open to anyone, a certain percentage of buyers and sellers are operating on the fringes of the law. In fact, online auctions are the source of most complaints to the FTC.

Like other Dotcons, Internet auction scams are variations of those perpetrated at auction sites for decades. The Internet adds a new dimension—anonymity. Neither the seller nor the buyer know who he or she is dealing with.

Anonymity fosters two kinds of Dotcons associated with auctions: frauds perpetrated by the seller on an unwitting buyer, and frauds perpetrated by buyers on an innocent seller.

Dotcons by the Seller

If you choose to participate in an online auction, you must realize that there are many ways that you can be defrauded. You can't see the other bidders. You can't inspect the merchandise before you purchase it, and you must pay for it before you get it.

When the auction starts, it's difficult to tell if the other bids are real, and even if you win the item and pay for it, there's no guarantee that it will arrive.

When it does arrive, it may not be what you expected, and when you try and get your money back, you may encounter an uncooperative seller in another state or country who can not be caught or prosecuted.

The Classic Auction Scam

I remember attending an auction in a small jewelry storefront on the boardwalk at Atlantic City in the early sixties. My fiancée was sporting a new diamond ring that I had just purchased after several months of shopping around learning about the price and value of "perfect stones." I had even looked through a microscope at the one she was wearing. A half-caret—small but perfect. I paid $478 for it.

A handsome well-dressed man stood at the door inviting us to have a seat amongst the half-dozen other "tourists" that were eagerly awaiting the auction to begin. We entered, and the man shut the door behind us. I remember thinking that there were still empty seats.

The well-dressed man went to the front of the room, introduced himself and then asked the members of the group where they were from–starting with me. When I told him I was a resident of a suburb of Philadelphia, he replied that he was too–and then quickly rattled off a description of a nearby township. Remarkably, his further questioning revealed that everybody else in the room was too! We all smiled at each other for a moment–such a friendly group.

When he asked who was a Phillies fan, all the other men in the group raised their hands. I didn't. Don't know why. I guess I just felt uncomfortable making the commitment. But after a few questions about the Eagles and Warriors, I was waving my hand with confidence.

The auction started with a casual presentation of a one and a half caret diamond guaranteed by the auctioneer to be a perfect stone. The bidders were suitably impressed as he walked through the small group.

My fiancée was notably aware of the difference between the rock being passed around and the comparative pebble I had given her. Much to my dismay, it was three times the size and just as perfect. I was sure it was worth several thousand.

The bidding started at a hundred dollars and then the auctioneer said, "one-fifty, two, two-fifty, three, three-fifty, four. Going once, going twice. Sold for four hundred dollars!"

"What?" I said under my breath. The bidding ended abruptly, and a smiling purchaser was taken to the back room where he emerged a few minutes later elated at the bargain that he had been able to acquire.

I was shocked but not elated. My fiancée glanced at the tiny ring on her finger and then up at me. I felt a little foolish having paid so much for a ring that was obviously inferior to the one that was just sold to the bidder who had the courage to raise his hand. No guts, no glory, I thought. I had four hundred bucks in my pocket. I could have seized that opportunity–if I just had the confidence. I was determined to do better.

The commotion settled and the auctioneer brought out another stone. This one was even larger than the last–a two caret solitaire, and of course, a perfect stone according to the auctioneer. Like the previous session, he passed it around and the other half-dozen people who had bid on the last one "ooh"d and "ah"ed in avaricious harmony.

The bidding started "One hundred, one-fifty, two-hundred, two-fifty, three, three-twenty-five," than a pause and, "going once, going twice." My hand shot into the air of its own free will and the words "three-fifty" came out of my mouth. I certainly wasn't going to let that incredible bargain get away. It was bigger than the one before. After all, I could sell it if I had to.

"Sold for three-hundred and fifty dollars!" No "going once, going twice", just "Sold for three-hundred and fifty dollars." Everybody clapped as the auctioneer shook my hand and took us into the back room to make the transaction.

Five minutes later I walked out and the room was empty. The auction was over; the "tourists" were gone, and I had a diamond and fifty bucks left in my pocket.

Shortly after we returned to Philadelphia, my fiancée took the new diamond ring to a jeweler, who was kind enough to let her see it through a jewelers glass. It was less than a caret, poorly cut to look larger, and cracked. The setting was thinly gold plated. According to the jeweler, it was worth less than a hundred bucks. When I read the guarantee, it said nothing about the size or quality of the stone. I had been taken. The whole thing was a set-up. The other people in the group were not tourists, they were shills.

Shilling

This is the term for fake bidders in an auction who are paid to cooperate with the auctioneer to influence the victim to bid on an item at the highest price possible. They instill a false confidence in the process by raising their hands eagerly early in the process, congratulating each other on their purchases, and encouraging the victim to bid. If the auction slows and the auctioneer believes he can squeeze more out of the victim, he simply gestures to the shill(s) who responds by raising the bid higher so that the victim ends up paying more for the item.

Conspiracies

On the Internet, the Dotcon artist and his partners can play you like a violin, because you can't see the people you're bidding against—if indeed there are other people. Shills operating in a conspiracy simply scratch each others' backs. They all have something to sell and they simply agree to bid on all items of sellers in the group regardless of what it is. Even if the site itself is legitimate, a Dotcon artist working with others has a significant advantage. If there are shills involved in the auction, you have literally no chance to get a fair deal.

Multiple Personalities

The sophisticated Dotcon artist doesn't have to risk a conspiracy, he can be all of the people bidding against you.

The anonymity of the auction allows the clever computer entrepreneur to log-on as several different people with several different identities. One identity, the seller, places the item for sale. The others bid on it. The bid goes slowly up to the minimum the Dotcon artist will accept and then awaits your entry. When you enter a bid, the anonymous bidders cautiously and carefully raise the bidding as long as you stay in.

The urgency of online auctions combines with the anonymity of the participants to influence you to bid higher when ordinarily you wouldn't. If bids come in on an item as the bidding is about to close on an item, you're likely to continue to bid on the item if it still remains a good value. In the end you may win, but you've paid more for the item than you would have. You might ask yourself why all these bids suddenly came in at the last minute. They were shills.

The Drop-out

Shilling helps the seller get more for the item by falsely entering bids. But in some cases, he (or one of his conspirators) is stuck with the last bid. Some online auctions provide a convenient method for the Dotcon artist to make sure you win. He simply drives the price up and then retracts his last bid at the last moment–leaving you paying more for the item than you expected.

The Name Change

Legitimate auction sites know about shilling and discourage it. Sellers that are caught by the operator of the auction site can be banned from the site. Of course that means little to the Dotcon artist. The anonymity of the online auction opens yet another crack in the integrity of the process–he merely signs on with a different name, or set of names.

Misleading Descriptions

One of the big differences between a live auction and an online auction is that you can't actually inspect the item. Like the cracked diamond in the gold-plated ring, when you buy something at an online auction you can't tell what you're actually getting because you can't see it with the naked eye. You must rely upon the description or picture of the item. Both can be fraudulent. The seller can both lie about the condition of the item as well as doctor the picture. Any elementary graphics program can be used to remove blemishes from an item or even add whatever logo or identification markings a victim might want to see to decide to buy the item online.

Deceptive Grading

Even if you're dealing with a reputable auction site and a seller who has an unblemished record, you nevertheless have a significant risk of not getting what you expected. "Beauty is in the eye of the beholder," and in an online auction the beholder is the person selling the item–not you. The words, "fair", "good", "excellent", "mint" mean different things to different people, and you can rest assured that the seller will describe his item using the best term he can.

Although this may sometimes be an honest mistake, often it is a deliberate ruse. For example, the Dotcom artist may know full well the item he is selling is in "Poor" condition, but he represents it as in "Good" condition *because he can get away with it.* You have no recourse based upon relative terms describing the object. No two people can be expected to share the same descriptive term about the condition of a used item, and for this reason it is difficult if not impossible to prosecute a Dotcon artist who represents a used item as in "Good" condition when in your opinion it is in "Fair", "Poor" or "Bad" condition.

Deceptive Relative Grading occurs so commonly that some auction sites encourage the use of "disinterested third parties" to appraise the item according to whatever standards are available. This provides some degree of protection to the buyer in the case of an out-and-out fraud; however, it still does not guarantee that the item is going to be in the condition that you expect.

Padding Shipping and Handling Fees

This is a legal method of extracting additional revenue from a sale made by mail, phone, or Internet. It's particularly common in online auctions. You struggle to win a bid of $10 for a rare comic book for your kid, and end up with an additional $5.99 tacked on for "Shipping and Handling." Of course, you don't notice when it comes third-class mail with forty cents of postage. The seller increased his net profits by well over 60%.

This is neither rare nor an accident. It is a deliberate misrepresentation of the costs to deliver the item for the purpose of increasing the revenue from the sale.

In fact, the practice has been commonly used for years in television offers for products selling for less than $20. Many mass marketers make their profits solely from the "Shipping and Handling Fees" they tack on to the purchase.

Offering Non-existent Items

The most blatant Dotcon is the auction of an item that doesn't exist. There is no item. You buy something online, pay for it by credit card, and it never arrives in the mail. This is mail fraud. It's a federal offense. Can it be that Dotcon artists can be so bold? Indeed according to the FTC, this kind of auction scam is one of the most common complaints they get. This is what it looks like:

1. You enter an online auction and win one of thirty "slightly used" , fully-loaded 700MHZ computers for $190. You're proud of yourself because some of the others went for $400 or more.

2. The auction requires you to pay for the item before its sent, so you type in your credit card number. You're elated when you get the e-mail response confirming the sale and the shipping date in about ten days.

3. Two weeks later, you're busy backing up the hard-drive on your old 150MHZ dinosaur when it strikes you that you've not seen the computer you bought. You send off an e-mail to the seller and get back a message saying it's been shipped. You wait another week and do it again. This time you get back a message saying the "E-mail address does not exist." Then you call the phone number and find that it's been disconnected.

    The whole thing was a con job. The "Stall" was an important part of the strategy. It gave the Dotcon artist enough time to credit the money from the "Charge" (and hundreds of others) and disappear while you patiently waited for the "Bargain" to arrive.

Selling Counterfeit Items

Another blatant fraud on the Internet is selling counterfeit items–Rolex's, Cartier's, Louis Vuitton purses, Beanie Babies, baseball cards, and other sports memorabilia.

The Internet is no different from the street vendor in this regard. The items are hard to distinguish from the real thing, and the person selling them to you disappears quickly after you pay him. You're better off with a street vendor. At least you can look at the product before you pay him, and you're pretty sure you're not getting a real Rolex.

Unfortunately, you don't get a chance to look at the Rolex sold at the online auction, and the other shills that are bidding make you think you are getting the real thing.

Once again, you are making your decision on the basis of a photograph, and it is unlikely that you will be able to tell the item is a fake by looking at it on your screen. Nobody can–except maybe the Dotcon artist, and he's made sure the picture doesn't show any distinguishing features.

If the Dotcon artist never actually claims the item is real, he can get away with it. *He will claim that he thought it was the real thing when he bought it, or that he never led you to believe it wasn't.*

Fencing Stolen Goods

Petty Theft and Burglary have shown no signs of abating in the 21st century. It is not uncommon to read in the paper of another house in your neighborhood being ransacked.

One of the biggest problems a burglar faces is how to get cash for his stolen goods. Traditionally pawnshops were the first stop a burglar made after he broke into your house and stole your jewelry and cash. But today when he steals your computer and printer, the pawnshop might not take them.

To whom does he turn? His friendly Dotcon artist who will buy them for a song, and then put them up for auction site using an anonymous name. In this regard, the anonymity of the seller, the inability to precisely identify the object, and the worldwide market makes the Internet an ideal environment for fencing stolen goods.

It is difficult for a law enforcement official in one state to track an object delivered in another, and it is unlikely that the buyer will recognize or report the crime. Even if the crime is discovered, an unwitting buyer will certainly not be prosecuted, and the anonymous seller can't be found.

There is one notable exception to this rule. If you knew or have reason to know that item was stolen, you could be considered an accomplice after the fact. This is the case with pirated software.

Pirated Software

A recent study of online auction sales estimated that over half the software sold at auction on the Internet was illegal. But nearly all the people who bought it thought it was simply used licensed software.

As the warning shows when you start a program, *you* are subject to copyright violation as well as the person who illegally copied it. And *you* are the easiest to prosecute. If it's installed on your computer and it belongs to someone else, *you have broken the law.*

Pirated software for sale on the Internet can be detected by a few key words used by the seller. You'll see descriptions such as :"CD-R Copy," or "Backup Copy" in the advertisement. Sometimes there will be nothing said.

If you end up with pirated software, you probably won't be happy with it. There may be large price difference between the price of a product and its auction price, but you may be getting exactly what you pay for. A product that is worth less than what you paid for it.

It might be infected with viruses, or it may not work at all. If it doesn't, you won't be able to get technical support. If it does, it's probably an older version, and you won't get upgrades from the manufacturer if it's an illegal copy.

Caveat Emptor on the Internet

Dotcons perpetrated on auction sites are anathema to the operators, who will do almost anything to stop them because they are ruining the public's confidence in e-commerce.

> *That is, they will do almost anything but take responsibility for losses suffered by their customers.*

The auction sites deflect any liability for illegal fraud by clearly stating that they are not responsible for the actions of sellers or the bidders, nor the condition or even the existence of the item itself. "Caveat Emptor," is sung in harmony by a chorus of Internet sites.

Site Precautions

The Internet auction sites have not ignored the problem, not at all; they are concerned. An early attempt to alleviate the problem of fraud is the publication of a "Feedback" system on the auction site—a forum where buyers and sellers can express their opinions about people on the site they have done business with.

The operators of the auction site claim that this facility, along with other "secure" measures they have taken, will help prevent fraud. They can point to instances where buyers have complained about a product not being delivered and the seller has been banned from the site, as well as instances where shills have been spotted and buyers have been banned from the site. Surely that should do it.

They know better. So should you. When a dedicated Dotcon artist is "banned" from the auction or receives enough bad feedback that he can't operate with impunity anymore, he changes his electronic identity, his username, and pops up again.

The Mutual Admiration Society

When Dotcon artists operate in a conspiracy, they not only team to inflate bids, but also to build each other's reputation on the Feedback page. They simply post glowing comments on the feedback pages of auction sites.

Buyer A will praise Seller B for the quality of the delivered merchandise. And Buyer B will praise Seller A for the help he provided over the phone in installing the software he bought from him on auction. Exponiate that little tag-team by a factor of five or so shills working together and you have a formidable stack of testimonials.

If you complain about a seller, your comment is likely to be buried in the heap of positive comments. This process is called "feedback padding" and like any other fraud is discouraged by auction site operators—*if and when* they recognize it. There is really no reason why they should. *Praise for sellers reflects back on the web-site itself. Even if it isn't true.*

Dotcons by the Buyer

You are at risk as a seller on an auction site for the same fundamental reason that you are at risk as a buyer: you don't know who you're dealing with. The user-names that appear as bids may be several people working together to defraud you leaving you with a fraction of what you expected to get from the auction. Or a single buyer may deceive you with several aliases.

And even if it was a fair deal, you may find yourself with a debit instead of a credit after you deliver the goods as described.

Deceptive Bidding

This Dotcon on an auction seller involves at least three bidders (or identities) working together. They buy the item you have for sale at a bargain price by driving any legitimate bidders out of the auction early in the bidding. It exploits the auction rule that allows bids to be withdrawn.

The three conspirators start the auction with an agreed price that they want to pay for your item. Normally it is far below the price you expected from a fair and honest auction. *But this isn't fair and honest!* One of the three has been selected to buy the item–the "designated buyer" in the Dotcon parlance.

When the designated buyer enters the bid that the group wants to win, the other two start a frenzy of bidding–so rapidly and high that any other legitimate bidder of your product becomes disillusioned and drops out of the auction–leaving the "designated buyer" as the last bid before the fake heated competition.

When the bidding is about to close, the two fake bidders both withdraw their bids at the last second. The bidding ends with the third conspirator winning the auction at precisely the price the group had decided upon.

You, the seller, are now obligated to sell the item at a fraction of the price it was worth.

Claiming Damage

This is a traditional scam that can be perpetrated by any buyer on an innocent seller. You ship the item in the condition advertised, but when the buyer receives the item, he claims it was damaged enroute. He expects you, the seller, to pay to repair the damage. He may even submit a fraudulent bill for the repairs that he made.

You're not in a bad position as the seller. The buyer really has little recourse if you choose to say no. He has already paid for the item by credit card, and the only thing he can do is dispute the payment with the credit card company. You're not home free though, because the buyer may refuse to pay and the credit card company may debit your account while the sale is "in dispute."

A good way to avoid this trick as a seller is to require the buyer to either purchase insurance or accept the liability for breakage during shipping.

Money-back Returns

This is a similar Dotcon job perpetrated by a buyer on the innocent seller. It is aggravated by the common practice of paying for items by credit card over the Internet.

In this scam the buyer gets your product, doesn't like it and wants his money back immediately. *He wants you to credit his credit card for the cost before he will return the item.*

You do, and he doesn't. If it's software, he makes a copy, installs it and then sends you back the original in the opened box. If it's a book, he reads it and sends it back. If it's anything else he could use, he uses it and sends it back. Sometimes he doesn't even send it back.

Protecting yourself in Online Auctions

Before you participate an online auction

- Read the rules well and observe the tempo of several sales. Some things that may seem unfair to you may be standard operating procedures. Others may show that he auction is operated carelessly, naively, or dishonestly.

When you have found something you wish to bid on

- Note the username of the seller.
- Check the feedback section of the auction site for comments about him.
- Reject sellers with negative comments.
- Check positive feedback from frequent bidders. See if the seller makes the same comments about them.
- Understand exactly what you are bidding on. Read the description and look at the image carefully.

Before the bidding starts

- Be sure you know just what the item is worth.
- Run a search on the Internet for similar items from retail web-sites and determine for yourself ahead of time the price that constitutes a better deal than you might find somewhere else.
- Add insurance, shipping and handling costs on large or expensive items. It might be cheaper locally.
- If you're planning to buy a collectible, be sure there is a text statement describing the item that is sufficient to confirm its value.
- If you need more specific details, ask the seller questions that can give you a better understanding of what you are buying.
- Set a maximum limit before the bidding starts.

During the bidding

- Cancel your bid immediately if you suspect a shill.
- Be ready for new flurries of bidding at the end of the auction.

After winning the bid

- If you have doubts about the seller or the process right after the bid, document the time, date and bidding sequence, and contact the auction site immediately.
- Immediately download the description and image of the item, should you be dissatisfied when the item is delivered.
- Don't buy the item if you spot fraud or shilling.

Arranging Payment

- If the seller is an individual, get a physical address and other identifying information to follow up if there is a problem.
- Check the seller's return policy. If he claims that all sales are final, tell him that you will not pay until you have inspected the item.
- Insure expensive items.
- Pay by credit card. You can dispute the charges if the goods are not as described.
- If you can't pay by credit card, use an escrow service.
- Insist upon an e-mail record of the transaction with a definite delivery date and any implied warranties or guarantees clearly specified.

After the Delivery

- Contact the seller and auction site directly if the item does not arrive. Record and retain the e-mail so that you have legal justification to dispute the payment.
- Check the item thoroughly when it arrives. If it does not meet the description in any way, immediately notify the seller and the auction site by e-mail.

After the Scam

- Advise the seller of discrepancies and attempt to negotiate an appropriate refund or return.
- Visit the buyer's feedback and give the seller an appropriate rating.
- If you cannot reach a settlement, make all correspondence by e-mail or certified mail so that you have legal evidence of the negotiations.
- Send an e-mail to the seller, with a copy to the FTC.

ONLINE SALES OFFERS

On March 2, 2000, three men were criminally charged in Philadelphia and one in San Diego for wire fraud when they sold Beanie Babies® on the Internet and then failed to deliver.

Online sales of products and services is perhaps the most fundamental promise of e-commerce. Although many of the goods and services are also sold in stores, the Internet offers a valuable way to search worldwide to find items that best meet your needs at the best price. In the broad spectrum of activities involved with sales, the process of "Shopping" can frequently be better done online with a computer than in person.

As "Online Shopping" has become commonplace, the Internet has adopted the taxonomy of the retail market place. Just as shoppers "visit" retail stores and "browse" through merchandise, so users of the Internet "visit" web-sites and "browse" for the best combination of quality and price. And when they find items they wish to purchase, they put them in a virtual "shopping cart", and "check out" with a credit card.

This similarity is not whimsy. It was designed specifically by marketing companies to make you feel comfortable in familiar surroundings–to reduce your anxiety about the new medium, to lower your defenses to entering your credit card information and generate revenues from a new and exciting source.

Of course, all of this is quite legitimate, and where would be as a nation without advertising? After all, "nothing happens until somebody sells something"…so they say.

Online Shopping Vs. Shopping

The problem is that "shopping online" is not the same as "shopping" at your local store: you know the salesman, or you can look him in the eye, you can inspect the merchandise, you can take the item home without paying any extra costs, and when you give the salesman your credit card number, he can confirm its you. These limitations have a severe effect on your ability to protect yourself from fraud: the merchandise you buy may not be as described, the person selling it may be deceiving you, you may be stuck with shipping and handling charges you didn't expect, and your credit card number and confirming data may be exposed to other people.

"Online shopping" per se is not dishonest, and every legitimate web-site is trying to make sure it stays that way, but as a consumer, you must realize that these basic limitations are like small cracks in the dike of e-commerce, and Dotcon artists are rushing to flood this new medium with fraud.

There is nothing fundamentally safer about buying things in person than buying them on the Internet. You can certainly be cheated just as easily by a con-artist in person as you can by a deceptive web-site. In fact many would argue that they feel safer dealing with a machine than a salesman!

Nevertheless, at least you've got the opportunity to look a salesman in the eye when you're buying something in person, complain in person to the manager of the store, and come back to return an item in person if it doesn't work as advertised. In other words, there are real people involved in conventional retail sales, and normally they're at a real building which is probably going to be there next week. The people and the store may in fact be no more trustworthy than the Internet site, but at least you can find out before you get stuck.

In other words, you wouldn't buy the fake Beanie Babies from a retail store in the first place. If you were gypped, you could go back to the store for a refund, but when you can't inspect the Beanie Baby and you have to pay for it before you get it, you are at a severe disadvantage.

Deception on the Internet

Dotcons can deceive you when you're shopping on the Internet by taking advantage of your inability to inspect the product before you pay for it. They advertise fabulous products or services, obtain payment, and disappear without providing the promised goods or services.

Because your decision to buy something on the Internet involves reading a textual description, looking at an image, or listening to a sound, the deception can take any of these forms.

False Advertising

The advertisement can be outright false, describing and a picture of something that is not the item that will be delivered, or it could be misleading-omitting important information or implying something that's a lie—a computer payment plan for "$0 Down" that you find involves a "$95 dollar set-up charge" when you have almost completed checking out! Misleading claims can also be unsubstantiated. Dotcons can easily sell obsolete 300MHZ computers by simply changing the L.E.D on the front to read 700MHZ, take a digital image of it, and the buyer will never know until his applications run slowly.

Faked Testimonials

Testimonials are faked or shilled. " 'Absolutely the best cigar I've ever smoked', says WJC of Little Rock Arkansas" is one of many short statements extolling the virtues of a product. Ask yourself if you've ever written to a cigar manufacturer just to say that it was the best cigar you've ever smoked. Neither did WJC. He's either a friend of the web-site operator, or is getting something from the web-site operator, or "is" the web-site operator.

Invalid Warranties

By law, warranties must be available before purchase for consumer products that cost more than $15. If the ad mentions a warranty on a product that can be purchased on the Internet, it must either publish a warranty or tell you how to get a copy of it. Legitimate sites encourage access to any guarantees, disclosures, disclaimers, and proof of any claims, because they contribute to sales. Dotcons don't. They prominently post phrases like "Money-back Guarantee" all over the product page or the order sheet, but the actual wording of the guarantee is difficult to find because it is hidden several clicks deep in the bowels of the logic structure. If they have to produce it, they will, and you can be sure it will limit their liability far beyond what the headline led you to believe.

Denying Responsibility

Although sellers themselves are responsible for claims they make about their products and services, web-site designers are also liable for making or disseminating deceptive representations. When you state that the product you received didn't meet the specifications of the advertising on the web-site. The web-site will claim they didn't make the product, and the manufacturer will claim they didn't advertise the product. This dodge is a Dotcon.

One of the classic ploys of the con man is to deny responsibility when confronted by an irate consumer. Illegitimate sites websites do this because they are not concerned about their reputation. They're not in business for the long run, and they are eager to get on to the next sale. If you are met with delays that just don't seem right. They aren't.

Fake Shipping and Handling

This is an old fraud that continues to survive because it's perfectly legal to do and easy to overlook. It was discussed earlier because it frequently occurs at auction sites. It's also common in mass sales of low-priced items where the shipping and handling costs constitute a large percentage of the gross revenue from the sale. A computer selling for $1000 that costs $40 to ship may be expensive, but a book selling for $10 that costs $3.72 to ship is probably a scam that is increasing the Dotcons annual profits by 30% or more.

You can see this in action every day on TV when special offers are made for generic products at prices that are clearly below the retail price of their brand name cousins. Products that sell for $15 in the store are offered for $9.95–but if you look closely you can see the "Add $5.99 for S & H".

You'll find the same scheme on the Internet where the costs for shipping and handling do not appear until after you have completed shopping and are ready to "check out." Sometimes you'll find that you end up paying more for the items than if you bought them at the store.

Stalling

When you buy a product from a local merchant, you can look at it, pay for it, and take it home. Legitimate e-commerce merchants aim to duplicate this process online; thereby helping you to feel confident and satisfied with your purchase.

The Federal Trade Commission also helps. The FTC requires the order to be shipped within 30 days unless another time is specified. If you don't receive your order within that time, the FTC requires that you be given the option of accepting the delay or canceling your order and receiving a prompt refund.

Fraudulent sales schemes on the Internet exploit the time-span between the purchase and receipt of the item. If the item you ordered does not arrive, or it is not what was advertised, it is possible that you are dealing with a Dotcon. The delay may be deliberate–giving the Dotcon enough time to process credit card charges from many victims, collect the money, and then disappear before any complaints surface.

If you don't get the product within the time specified or you're not satisfied with it then according to the Fair Credit Billing Act you may dispute the charge and withhold payment on the disputed amount while the charge is in dispute.

E-mail the billing address on the web-site and describe what happened. They must acknowledge your complaint by mail or e-mail in writing within 30 days after receiving it and they must reach an agreement with 90 days after receipt of your e-mail.

Buying Illegal Items

Crime doesn't pay! At least not when you're the criminal. This Dotcon involves the fake sale of thinly disguised illegal items on the Internet–things like "Duplicate Social Security Cards", guns, explosives, prescription drugs, pirated software, and other clearly counterfeit merchandise. They are advertised on the web-site, you pay for them in cash so that you can't be traced, and they are never delivered.

The Dotcom relies on the fact that you won't complain to the authorities when you don't get the item or you find that it is worthless for your nefarious purpose.

This is a near perfect Advanced Fee Dotcon that has likely claimed thousands of victims under the age of 21. For example, you might try to obtain a fraudulent document (like a drivers license) or item that is illegal for you to purchase in your state (or country). When the product doesn't arrive, you have no recourse. You won't report the fraud, because you would incriminate yourself. There is no phone number to call and the address the cash went to is in a foreign country.

This fraud was discovered through independent research, because there are no government statistics. A teenager told me that she had found a site offering fake California driver's licenses with altered birth dates. When she sent a $50 bill in an envelope to an address in Canada, she received nothing. Of course there was no phone.

Search for "Fake SSN's", "Fake ID's", "University Degrees". You'll find dozens of attractive offers all with the same characteristics: they are selling a product used to defraud others, they are asking for cash up front, and you rationalize the risk as necessary for you to obtain the illegal product. Some of these offers of "illegal" products may themselves be legitimate; although there is little reason for them to be so.

False Promotions

"Buy now and receive a state-of-the-art graphics program absolutely free." This is an adaptation of a classic advertising ploy that implies you are going to get a special discount (or a free purchase) of an item if another is purchased. On the surface there is nothing wrong or illegal about the offer. The scam is that the item you are getting free is worth little or nothing.

Freeware and shareware add a new deceitful dimension to this traditional scheme when it is perpetrated on the Internet. Because the product that is offered "free" is in fact free anyway, the Dotcon artist is not lying—merely misleading.

But it is nevertheless illegal! The FTC claims that advertisements like *"buy one, get one free"* require that the free item is something of value and that the consumer will pay nothing for the one item and no more than the regular price for the other.

Computer Components

The price of computers is in steady decline as the rapid pace of technology obsoletes one chip after another. It should be no surprise to find bargains on the internet. The Dotcon happens when they aren't bargains at all. They are missing expensive components that you expected.

The devil's in the details. *The picture will show a computer, monitor, and speakers, but the description will omit the monitor and the sound board.* Look carefully and you will also find the shipping and handling charges seem a little excessive. When you add the components you will need you may find that the system offers no more than your local computer store—and you can always take it back there.

Internet Contracts with Computers

This is a legitimate offer but deceptive in its value. The offer is a low initial price on a computer together with a mandatory contract with an Internet service. Ordinarily this might be an attractive offer if you needed to go online anyway. Where's the con? Not in the computer. It's in the contract!

Check the contract duration and the price you are going to pay for this service. If the service is not one of the leaders, you may have to connect with a long-distance number. Perhaps the service is notably inferior than another you might have chosen. There might be a balloon payment somewhere in the payment plan, or it might be expensive to cancel? There's a reason why this bargain is being offered this way. And that reason might be worth more than the savings you're getting on the computer.

Risky Rebates

These are legitimate sales offers that require you to pay the full-price up-front for an item and then to "mail-in" a rebate to get a portion of your money back.

The Internet adds a dimension of risk to this legitimate offer, because the rebate normally comes from another company. It can be delayed for months or not delivered at all, but when you contact the Internet web-site, they will tell you that they are not responsible for the loss. It is also possible that there was no other company, or rebate. A Dotcon site may have just retained the money.

Fake Web-sites

Most Dotcons are simply modern adaptations of classic scams, but the "Fake Web-site" is unique to the wonderful world of e-commerce. It is done by misleading people to go to a counterfeit web-site where the high-rate of "hits" will then allow the Dotcon artist running the site to charge premium prices for the banner ads displayed.

The Federal Trade Commission recently announced it is going after web-sites that redirect you from legitimate web-sites to pornographic sites. According to the FTC, the perpetrators made exact copies of up to 25 million Web pages posted by legitimate organizations and inserted commands to automatically go to their site.

This is a sophisticated bit of programming that demonstrates how far the Dotcon artist can and will go to deceive you for profit. You can see it happen when your screen flashes and a window appears that has no relevance to the web-site you selected. In the most severe cases, you may find that you cannot rid yourself of the unwanted window, because the Dotcon artist has deactivated the navigation keys on your browser while you are viewing the offending page.

Fake University Degrees

There are dozens of web-sites that offer you the opportunity to be granted an advanced degree or certification with very little effort. These are electronic versions of the same kinds of ads you will find in pulp magazines.

In some cases, they state that the degrees are from "accredited" institutions. The catch is that the word "accredited" has a different meaning to the web-site operator than it might have to the person you plan to show it to (like a new employer). If the institution is not recognized by the U.S. Department of Education then the degree may be worthless.

Like other Dotcons the Internet aggravates the scope and impact of the scam, because the worldwide scope makes it more difficult to determine whether or not the degree has any value, or if indeed the institution even exists. The U.S. Department of Education does not accredit foreign institutions, so it is possible that a degree from "Cambridge College" might be legitimate. Determination of the validity of a university degree is beyond the scope of this book, but these are some of the red flags that the federal government would have you look for:

- Promises that no one is turned down.
- Degrees that can be obtained for present knowledge or life experience.
- Advertisements that allow one to call at any time of the day of the week including holidays.
- Tuition is charged on a per-degree basis rather than credit hours.
- No designated professor with whom you can speak.
- Post office box numbers instead of addresses.

Protecting against Online Sales Frauds

Online sales is a cornerstone of e-commerce, but the novelty, popularity, and widespread scope of the Internet has created a fertile field for Dotcon artists. The federal government and the Internet industry are working hard to limit your vulnerability to these kinds of online scams, but like any other business transaction, the final responsibility for protecting yourself lies with you. You, the buyer, must beware. These are some general tips that will help you:

- Try to deal with established companies with business addresses and phones as well as e-mail addresses.
- Avoid small "companies" with free e-mail addresses, which can be anonymous.
- Be cautious of all foreign companies, Antigua, St. Kitts, Costa Rica, even "safe" places like Canada, England, and Australia.
- Ignore items that appear unsolicited in your mailbox.
- Trust your intuition. If you have a funny feeling about an item, don't buy it.
- If you do decide to buy from someone new, don't ever conduct business with an anonymous person.
- Verify the business name , address, and phone number before you buy anything.
- Use a credit card to purchase online. Your liability is limited and you can dispute the purchase.
- Don't ever send a payment to a post-office box.
- Download and retain the description, image, and guarantee of the item. If the item is not as advertised, you have documentation for legal recourse.
- If you are not satisfied when the item when it arrives, or even worse, it doesn't arrive, then e-mail the web-site who sold it to you. Retain the e-mail and all others.

- Keep notes if you call the company by phone.
- If you are unable to resolve the problem with the company, send them an e-mail with a copy to the Federal Trade Commission and the US Postal Service.

SWEEPSTAKES AND PRIZE DOTCONS

During 1999, the Federal Trade Commission received more than 10,000 complaints about sweepstakes and prize promotions.

The online sweepstakes or prize Dotcon looks the same as it's postal predecessor: *"Congratulations, Mrs. Jones, you just won prizes worth $5,000!"*

The Internet dramatically increases the scope and persuasiveness of this scam. Thanks to the marvels of the Information Age, it's easy for the Dotcon artist to get your name and those of millions of others, correlate all sorts of information about you and then send a bulk e-mail that totally convinces you that this is a personal message.

Sweepstakes and Prizes by E-mail

Any unsolicited e-mail telling you that you just won a prize is probably a scam!

If there's truly a lot of money involved, then you will be contacted in person or by registered mail–certainly not with Spam.

The Dotcon in some schemes is that the "prize" isn't worth what they say it is, and you're going to have to do something to get it–pay a processing fee, attend a sales seminar, or provide personal information that is of value to the sender. Whatever it is, the "prize" may cost you hundreds of dollars in up-front fees, service charges, or your privacy—and then never arrive. Or the sender may in fact send your "prize" to stay within the letter of the law, but the prize won't be worth what you thought it was. A "genuine diamond ring" the size of a pinhead, or a "Fabulous Las Vegas Vacation" consisting of one night in a motel and a book of "Two-for-One" coupons.

You will also get seemingly harmless Spam from other Dotcons asking you to *enter* contests or sweepstakes–with no obligation or risk. The Dotcon is to get you to reveal enough information about yourself that they can sell it or use it themselves for more Dotcons. If you fill it out, you probably won't get a prize in the mail, but you will be sure to get more junk mail, unwelcome phone calls, and Spam.

Here's an example of a happy prizewinner who's about to be scammed:

Subj: You are a Winner!
From: ComputersRUs@ix.netcom.com (ComputersRUs)
You're the first person from our list of thousands, to win a FREE US Robotics 56K bps with new x2 technology, modem from Computers R Us! Our growing area has nearly doubled its popularity over the US in the past year, just from these contests alone! In order for you to receive your FREE 56K x2 bps modem from our company.

Name: _____
Address: _____
City: _____ State: _____ Zip: _____
Telephone Number: (___) ___-____
Also what version you need IBM or MAC: _____

We will need you to pay for the Shipping and Handling with your Credit Card Only. (To let us know that your 18 or over and also for safety reasons)

Name _____

Shipping Address _____

City _____

State _____

FedEx Charges   Two Day $12

Credit Card Type: VISA, MasterCard, DiscoverCard American Express

Credit Card Number: _____

Expiration Date: _____

Skill Dotcons

Another popular scam that is uniquely suited for the interactive nature of the Internet is the "skill contest".

In the 1980's you may recall getting offers in the mail to win hundreds of dollars by completing a cross-word puzzle, figuring out a simple word puzzle, or finding the mistakes in the picture. Today you are offered the opportunity to win thousands of dollars by outwitting, or outmaneuvering an opponent in an interactive computer game. Looks like fun, What could be the harm?

The scam is to get you to pay to continue to participate in the game or be eligible to win the prize. When the scam's done, you either lose the contest, or you've paid more than the prize was worth.

You can recognize this scam, because it's psychologically rewarding. Whatever it is you're asked to do, you win! Then you are asked to send a small donation or fee in to continue in the competition. And then you win again!

Once you've sent your money in, you're "hooked". The questions get harder and the entry fees get steeper. Finally you (and everybody else) loses. Occasionally you get a booby prize in consolation for your participation. In this case, it's appropriate!

If you are tempted to enter a contest of this kind, check the web-site to see if it's described fully according to law. The Deceptive Mail Prevention and Enforcement Act requires them to post the terms, rules and conditions of the contest, how many rounds of the contest you must complete to win, and when and where the winner will be announced.

Foreign Lotteries

You've probably taken a chance at your state lotto. Why not take a chance on the e-mail or the web-site offering you a share in a pool of tickets for a lottery in Canada? The e-mail promises much better odds. This scam has been going around for years–perpetrated by mail. The U.S. Postal Inspection Service claims that thousands of U.S. citizens have been bilked out of millions of dollars by fraudulent foreign lotteries.

Purchasing foreign lotteries are illegal, because federal law prohibits mailing payments to purchase any ticket, share, or chance in a foreign lottery. This particular statute is questionable, because you're not mailing the payments to this web-site; you are making a credit card purchase. But whether it's legal or not is less relevant than whether or not you're about to be Dotconned!

Like other Off-shore Dotcons these companies are not covered by U.S. Federal law. Even worse they are likely to be unregulated by the government of the country in which they are located. In some cases, you may receive a confirmation by e-mail. Otherwise you'll never see any evidence that lottery tickets were purchased on their behalf. *You have absolutely no legal recourse!*

Avoiding Sweepstakes Dotcons

Sponsors of legitimate contests identify themselves prominently and don't require you to pay or buy something to enter or improve your chances of winning. If you have to pay to receive your "prize," it's not a prize at all. Legitimate promoters also provide you with an address or toll-free phone numbers, and bona fide offers clearly disclose the terms and conditions of the promotion in plain English, including rules, entry procedures, and usually, the odds of winning. So the next time you get an e-mail telling you "it's your lucky day," you might consider the following precautions:

- Read the fine print.
- Don't agree to attend a meeting to win an "expensive" prize.
- Don't pay to win or enter. You cannot be required to purchase goods or services or to pay fees to win or collect a prize.
- Keep your credit card and bank information to yourself.
- Don't give bank information or social security number to someone who claims it's needed to verify your eligibility or to "deposit winnings" in your account.
- Don't send a web-site money for taxes. Only the government collects taxes on prize winnings.
- Request that your name be removed from the e-mail lists.

VIRUSES

A computer virus is a program that copies itself and that can "infect" other programs by modifying or deleting them or files they need to work. They cause strange effects–magically appearing or disappearing pictures, text, sounds, memory, and worst of all–your personal files.

The Melissa virus is a good example of an infection of Microsoft Word. You catch it by opening an infected Microsoft Word document. It can be attached to an e-mail, or passed from one computer to another by floppy disk. Once your computer is infected, your Microsoft Word program will act up–running out of memory, changing function key operations, and spewing random text into your documents.

Catching the Virus

You might receive an e-mail with a request to "Read the attached file" or "Check out the babe in the picture." All you have to do is click it and you've caught it.

When the virus is attached it to a persuasive piece of Spam and sent it to millions of recipients, asking them to send it to millions more, the damage is enormous *even if only a small percentage of the recipients are infected.*

The ploy is simple and easy to fall for: the e-mail message simply implores you to open the attachment. When you do, the virus attaches itself to your computer and does its work

Spreading the Virus

Viruses borrow their name from single cell infections that spread from host to host. The Human Immune-deficiency Virus (HIV) being the most dreaded. But computer viruses are not biological accidents. They are small, clever pieces of executable code that are created by computer programmers whose motives include profit, malicious mischief, and infamy.

The intent of "Doctor Doom" and the "Trojan Horseman" differs little from the "Unibomber" and "Boston Strangler", only the results. They both derive pleasure from the worldwide notoriety they gain by wreaking havoc.

The first viruses were prank programs written in machine language and limited to the type of computer that could run their program. But now everyday word processing programs have macro languages provide a powerful host for viruses.

Microsoft Word allows you to write simple programs to do repetitive tasks—for example to open, copy, and close files. "Doctor Doom" uses it to embed a virus in an innocent looking ".doc" file to *delete* files—yours.

But that's certainly not all. The effects of a virus are limited only by the imagination (or sick humor) of the Dotcon artist who creates it. They can be set off by any combination of keys, mouse clicks, dates, or times, and they can cause pictures, words, sounds to occur, erase current memory to cause errors in certain programs as they are running, erase important documents, or wipe out your entire hard drive.

Symptoms of Infection

Most viruses are designed to avoid detection and try not to call attention to themselves. You are normally unaware that you have contracted a virus until you start up the infected program or reboot your computer.

The worst kinds of viruses delete your personal files. This is a real disaster If you've not backed it up recently, A common feature in Virus protection is to look for the word "del" and the sequence of characters "*.*" , "*.doc"

Another similar kind deletes important files in your \Windows and \Program Files directories–files with suffices like ". exe" and ".DLL". This then causes you to reinstall Windows and/or the software programs you have installed.

The most common kind of virus works on your Microsoft Word program by altering one or more of the files it needs to work properly. For example, you can't save a document, your files are way too big, strange words appear in your letters, or your hard drive light stays on most of the time.

Another deadly kind of virus works on the system files and affect all programs–not just Microsoft Word. They steal memory so that none of your applications seem to work right, or they intercept and omit keystrokes, mouse clicks, or combinations of letters. You end up buying a new keyboard or mouse before you know you've been affected.

The Family of Viruses

Like their biological equivalents, different viruses do different damage in different ways.

- A TROJAN HORSE is a program that performs as advertised, but does something unknown to the user.
- A WORM is a TROJAN HORSE that copies itself to other computers when it runs

- A FILE INFECTOR is a program that attaches another piece of code to an ordinary program file.
- A STEALTH INFECTOR is that operates without detectable changes to the files it infects. The programs operate difficulty but the files appear the same to Anti-Virus programs.
- A COMPANION is a STEALTH virus that doesn't change the target program, it simply replaces it with another one of the same size and date.
- A POLYMORPHIC INFECTOR does different things at different times when it infects a file, making it difficult for the user to detect as a virus.
- A FAST INFECTOR spreads to both programs that are operating and files they use.
- A SPARSE INFECTOR infects programs at random intervals to hide its presence.

Virus Prevention

The best way to protect yourself against viruses is to use Virus Protection programs. These are available from many companies. They detect viruses by finding identifying characteristics in specific kinds of files. They must be constantly updated, and even the best will not assure 100% protection. So even if you are using a virus protection program, it's still a good idea to considering the following procedures:

After you've installed a virus protection program, don't open any attachments from people you don't know, and only open the ones from people you do know if the attachment is described in the message itself. The latter is important because some viruses attach themselves to e-mails without the sender knowing it. Your friend could have sent you a perfectly legitimate e-mail with an attached virus and never knew it. Here are some other ways to avoid infection:

- Scan floppy disks you get from someone else.
- Never download files from strangers! If you receive an e-mail with an attached file, do NOT download the file unless you know the sender.
- If you choose to open an attachment and suspect it contains a virus, scan it before you open it
- Don't click on hyperlinks in e-mail from strangers!
- Don't ever run an ".exe" file that is attached to an e-mail that you don't recognize.

SPAM

"Spam" is a slang term for unsolicited e-mail that arrives in your mailbox from someone you don't know concerning something you weren't interested in–an answer for which you had no question.

Spam is the electronic equivalent of junk mail, and the impact on the receiver is the same: it wastes your time, distracts you from more important mail, and frequently defrauds you. The announcement that you just won a "Fabulous Las Vegas vacation" from a real estate developer you never heard of is Spam.

Flooding your computer with Spam is just as legal as filling your mailbox with junk mail. It's unethical, but there's no law against it–unless the offer itself is deceptive or illegal. In fact, major e-commerce services routinely send out bulk e-mail to all their members. They claim that this is not Spam, because you have a "prior relationship with the seller"; that is, you know who it is coming from.

To their credit, the legitimate organizations that send bulk e-mail will be happy to remove you from their list if you object to the nature of the e-mail you are getting. Illegitimate Dotcons won't.

Modus Operandi

Spam is generated by businesses or individuals by sending the same offer in an e-mail message to millions of people. The objective is to entice a small percentage to respond to the offer, no matter how outlandish. The offer itself could be a warped joke, a simple fraud of a few dollars on a hundred people, a major fraud of only a few, or in the worse case a malicious and dangerous virus that shuts down e-commerce at the cost of millions, even billions of dollars.

The common characteristic is that the e-mail reach a wide audience from which there will inevitably be a small percentage of suckers.

Sending Spam

Spam proliferates because Spam campaigns are so simple and inexpensive to execute. Simple computer programs that send Spam are available for less than a hundred dollars. More sophisticated ones that will customize the message for each recipient are a little more expensive, and even state-of-the -art program with features that will defeat your Spam filters are only slightly more. Sending Spam is cheap.

Sending Spam is also easy to do. The Dotcon artist merely creates a message that will solicit a response and sets up his computer to deal with the responses. Then he cranks up the Spam program, selects the list of millions he has bought, clicks the mouse on "Send", and goes to lunch. Within a few minutes, you have one more piece of junk mail.

E-mail Lists

Lists to send it to are also relatively inexpensive. Search for "E-mail lists" or "Bulk E-mail" and see for yourself. According to the quality of information about each of the people on the list, an eager entrepreneur can easily afford to buy a lists of thousands—even millions. It's likely that your name is on one of them.

Hyperlinks in Spam

E-mails can do very little to harm your computer unless you open an attached document. Websites however are more powerful, because they can capture your e-mail address and other data from cookies on your hard drive.Getting you from an e-mail to a Dotcon website is a particularly rewarding accomplishment for the Dotcon artist.

The Dotcon artist gets you from his Spam to his site by encoding a simple hyperlink in the Spam message. This then leads you to his website and provides a better degree of access to your computer...and your psyche.

Why me?

Your name is a penny, nickel, or dime in the currency of the Information Age. If you're on the Internet, you've got an e-mail address, and your name, address, and even phone number are associated with it. These eventually end up in a database and sold on a list to anybody who wants to contact you.

Legitimate sites claim to have a privacy policy that states they do not sell, rent, give, or otherwise provide addresses to outside parties. They don't need to. Your address is easily available to just about anybody who wants it. And the more people know about you, the more Spam you will get.

If you've ever entered financial data, there will be more people who will contact you. Medical information, even more. Been in a chat room and talked about your arthritis, won't be long until your getting junk mail for "Herbal Cures".

Looking for a job, filled out a resume online–you'll get lots and lots of Spam. Every word you entered is a keyword in some marketers target market.

Why you? If you're on the Internet, then you're on a list. If you're on the Internet a lot, you're on a lot of lists.

Opt-out Sites

A Dotcon on Spam, these are web pages that offer to protect you by having your e-mail address removed from mail lists. Instead they put you on another list. They invite you to enter your e-mail address and promise to forward it at no charge to a selected list of advertisers and List vendors with a legal-sounding "Remove me from list" demand.

Ask yourself why they are doing this for free? The answer is they are selling your information to competitors of the list you were on. *You go off one list and on another. An advertisers dream…and your nightmare.*

Chain Spam

Chain Spam describes e-mail messages that duplicate the result of chain letters that have been sent in the mail for years. You receive a letter in the mail that asks you to make copies of the letter and send them to your friends, asking them to do the same thing. The intent is to spread the message of the letter exponentially, one person sends the letter to ten of his friends, who each send the letter to ten of their friends, ad infinitum. A million people receive the letter by the sixth iteration.

This process is particularly effective by e-mail because the process of copying and retransmitting the message is effortless and free. When you receive chain e-mail, you don't have to Xerox a dozen copies, address each one, and pay the postage. Rather you need only forward the letter as an attachment to all of the people in your address book, and copy the sender. Chain Spam therefore travels quicker and farther than regular chain letters.

Chain Spam is more difficult to stop than normal Spam because the volume of messages emanate from hundreds and thousands of different sources. A single person or business sending out a thousand copies of unsolicited e-mail can be identified by his Internet Service Provider. *But 111 people sending out ten e-mails each probably won't concern the different ISP's.*

Chain Spam can be sent for profit, malice, or whimsy. The Dotcon artist either get information about you that he can sell, damage your computer or reputation, or just get a laugh.

Chain Spam for Profit

The old-time chain letter asked you to send money to somebody, but in Information Age every bit of your personal data has value. Today, the Dotcon artist uses Chain Spam to gather data about you to sell to others. It could vary from just getting your e-mail address to making a list of your affinity contacts. In either case, the Dotcon artist is making a list of people in the chain and then selling it to others.

This is accomplished by directing you to be sure to "Copy" the original sender when you forward the e-mail to your "friends." Each time the e-mail is sent, the original sender gets a copy.. A chain Spam that makes it through seven iterations, would theoretically have information (or a contribution) from 1,111,111 people and 11,111,111 e-mail addresses—that would then be put on a list that will be sold by the originator of the Spam.

Read this and see if you can figure out what's going to happen when you tearfully forward it to all your friends.

> > > Little Jessica Mydek is seven years old and is
> > > suffering from an acute and rare case of
> > > cerebral carcinoma. This condition causes severe
> > > malignant brain tumors and is a terminal illness.
> > > The doctors have given her six months to live.
> > > As part of her dying wish, she wanted to start a
> > > chain letter to inform people of this condition and
> > > to tell people to live life to the fullest
> > > and enjoy every moment, a chance that she will never
> > > have. Furthermore, the American Cancer Society
> > > and several corporate sponsors have agreed to
> > > donate three cents toward continuing cancer
> > > research for every new person that gets forwarded
> > > this message.
> > > Please give Jessica and all cancer

> \> > > victims a chance. Forward this message to all
> \> > > your friends
> \> > > BE SURE TO SEND A COPY OF THE E-MAIL
> \> > > to American Cancer Society at ACS@ANYDOMAIN.COM

Figured it out yet? Right! ACS isn't the American Cancer Society! It's a Dotcon artist starting a business of his own—selling information about you and your friends. He's putting together a mailing list of "fresh", "validated", "guaranteed" e-mail addresses that he's going to sell for a couple of cents a name—again, and again, and again.

Whimsical Spam

Few people pick up the phone and call all their friends when they hear a good joke! But the Internet is different. If something strikes you funny, you can share the humor with your friends with a few clicks of a mouse.

Have you ever received a peculiar e-mail that doesn't ask you to copy anybody or do anything. You either scratch your head and ask yourself why anyone would send it to you, or heartily laugh and forward it to somebody else who might appreciate it. It's all according to whether or not you get the joke.

You may recall the Internet traces its roots back to academia, and as recently as the 1980's, commercial use of the new medium was discouraged by the scientists and students using it. It was a forum for arcane scientific discussion, and much of that discussion was, and remains, wry humor.

Last year I received an official looking press release attached to an e-mail from a source I couldn't recognize. My first impulse was to delete it, but I read it instead.

It announced that *Microsoft had just bought the Catholic Church, and had just established a new division to sell religious software and computer services from the Vatican to Catholics all over the world.*

Bill Gates had allegedly said that this merger of two great organizations called WinPope 2000 was a religion upgrade for the 21st Century providing the capabilities for online mass, interactive confessions, chatrooms featuring the Pope, and the auction of indulgences to reduce the time you spent in Purgatory.

Some people, mostly Catholics, thought this was funny enough to pass on to their friends. Others didn't, and protested the libel and waste of resources. Perhaps the most pernicious effect of the illegal Spam on the Internet is that we're becoming afraid to laugh at the legal e-mails.

Virus Hoaxes

A virus hoax is a warning sent by Spam warning you of a virus. Even the newest user of the Internet is aware of the danger of viruses; although most people are unsure exactly what they are, what they do, and how they are spread.

Viruses were discussed earlier, but the fear of these viruses has spawned a new Spam Dotcon, the virus hoax—a fake warning message about some virus or another. They arrive as a Chain Spam and encourage you to stop the worldwide damage by forwarding the e-mail to everyone in your address book.

You believe many of them because they are written in technical jargon that you don't understand, and then you dutifully pass it on–making your contribution to society. The message is in an attachment, you have simply spread it. In fact it is either a prank or a virus itself that relies on your fear of viruses to spread it. In either case don't open the attachment.

The example below is carefully crafted to remove all doubt that you will be helping mankind by simply forwarding it to all your friends, who mail distribute it to all their friends. And they will all have SAFEDEMO.EXE (the virus itself) on their hard-disk.

>>>DANGER!!! VIRUS ALERT!!! THIS IS A NEW TWIST.
>>>SOME CREEPOID SCAM-ARTIST IS SENDING OUT
>>>A DESIRABLE SCREEN-SAVER (THE BUD FROGS).
>>>BUT IF YOU DOWN-LOAD IT, YOU'LL LOSE EVERY THING!!!!!
>>>YOUR HARD DRIVE WILL CRASH!!
>>>BE CAREFUL. PLEASE DISTRIBUTE THIS TO AS
>>>MANY PEOPLE AS POSSIBLE..THANX
>>>HERE'S A SAFE VERSION OF WHAT FROGGIE LOOKS LIKE!
File: SAFEDEMO.EXE (24643 bytes)

Some other virus hoaxes are more obvious. The difference between the two is that they don't have any attachment for you to open or read.

FREUDIAN VIRUS

Your computer becomes obsessed with marrying its own motherboard.

PBS VIRUS

Your computer stops every few minutes to ask for money.

ELVIS VIRUS

Your computer gets fat, slow and lazy, then self-destructs—only to resurface at shopping malls and service stations across rural America.

OLLIE NORTH VIRUS

Causes your printer to become a paper shredder.

SEARS VIRUS

Your data won't appear unless you buy new cables, power supply and a set of shocks.

JIMMY HOFFA VIRUS

Your programs can never be found again.

KEVORKIAN VIRUS
Helps your computer shut down as an act of mercy.

IMELDA MARCOS VIRUS
Sings you a song (slightly off key) on boot-up, then subtracts money from your Quicken account and spends it all on expensive shoes it purchases through Prodigy.

STAR TREK VIRUS
Invades your system in places where no virus has gone before.

HEALTH CARE VIRUS
Tests your system for a day, finds nothing wrong and sends you a bill for $4,500.

LAPD VIRUS
It claims it feels threatened by the other files on your PC and erases them in "self-defense."

Protecting yourself against Spam

There is no law against Spam. There is, however a law that makes it illegal to send unsolicited advertising by fax. This law (47 USC 227) passed several years ago when the taxpayers complained about their fax machines being flooded with useless junk mail.

The government's jurisdiction in Interstate Commerce made it possible to pass this law, because the data was flowing over a telephone line across state lines. It would therefore seem to be applicable to e-mail; however, attempts so far have failed in court.

The question remains as to whether the billion-dollar Internet companies that are based upon mass collection and distribution of data are going to invite the federal government into the business of regulating the Internet.

While you are waiting for this to happen, it might be a good idea to protect yourself. Here are some ideas:

- Change your E-mail address immediately. This is the surest and safest way of getting rid of Spam, and making it more difficult to target you for any scams. Just as your Social Security Number is the primary means for the government to identify you, your e-mail address is the primary reference of the Dotcon artist. You can't change your SSN, but you can change your e-mail address.

- Get another e-mail address just for newsgroups and mailing lists and ignore any mail you get from that address. If you're using a different address for personal mail then all mail in the former box is "unsolicited".

- Use anonymous e-mail addresses. This is a legitimate way of protecting your personal data. If they don't know anything else about you but your e-mail address, you're not as valuable to the advertisers and the list merchants.

- Set up your own mail system to screen messages that do not have a keyword, (your name or other identifier) in the Subject line, and then send them to a separate directory. Then send a message to your important e-mail contacts advising them to contact you that way.

- Ignore Spam. Don't even read it. Several years ago, this warning would have been conditional, but today the use of Spam is universally considered to be unethical in business transactions. This means that anybody using Spam is either incompetent, ill-informed, or dishonest.

- If you can't ignore it, don't ever respond to it. You do the spanner a favor if your complaint actually does get back, because you have just validated that your address exists. You're on another list.

- Don't click on hyperlinks in e-mail you receive from strangers.

- Do not buy *anything* from unsolicited advertising, especially if it seems to be a bargain. If it seems too good to be true, it probably is.
- Forward Spam to the domain of the return address with a demand that they stop it. Use abuse@domain and postmaster@domain.
- If you live in an enlightened state that has passed legislation against Spam, forward the Spam piece to the State Attorney General.

ASSET TRACERS

Have you received an e-mail from an "Asset Recovery" company claiming that they have identified money that the government owes you? Your initial reaction is to dismiss it as a fraud. Maybe, maybe not.

The government does in fact owe billions of dollars to citizens as a result of mistakes involving uncashed checks, non-refunded deposits, forgotten bank accounts & safe deposit boxes, abandoned stocks & bonds, unpaid insurance & retirement benefits, and a host of other financial assets.

The law declares assets to be "abandoned" after the owner fails to make a deposit or withdrawal on a bank account after a certain amount of time, apply for a benefit, insurance policy payout, credit or refund due, or holds uncashed any check, money order, or gift certificate.

The banks, insurance companies, employers, unions, brokerages, utilities, landlords, and retail stores that recognize these lapses are required to turn the unclaimed assets over to the "protective custody" of the government in a process called "escheat."

Legitimate "Asset Recovery" companies specialize in locating these owners of unclaimed and abandoned assets. They gather data about the asset and try to match it to the data they find out about you. When they find a match, they contact you with an offer to collect and deliver the money for a fee to be deducted from the amount the collect—normally a percentage of up to 25%.

Asset Recovery Dotcons work in two ways: a variation of the Advance Fee scam, and an identity theft that taps your bank account

Advanced Fee Asset Recovery Dotcon

The first scam looks perfectly legal. The illegitimate "Asset Recovery" company gains access to your personal data from an Internet marketing company and carefully crafts an e-mail that demonstrates an intimate knowledge of your past—thereby convincing you that they have genuine knowledge of a lost asset. For example, they may refer to a deceased relative or an old address or job, leading you to believe that they may indeed have knowledge of an asset worth claiming. They offer to research this claim for a small fee to be paid up-front. Of course, nothing is ever found. There are no assets to recover.

Asset Recovery from your Bank Account

The second version of the scam does in fact go after assets-*your current assets*. The Dotcon artist gets the information about your accounts and then simply swindles you.

There is no central database for unclaimed government assets, and each individual federal agency maintains its own records and researches data on a case-by-case basis. The government is authorized to reveal federal check issuance data under the provisions of the Freedom of Information Act.

Legitimate asset retrieval companies may ask you to confirm account numbers in order to collect the payment amounts from the federal agencies. Illegitimate companies ask for this information without instead of confirming it.

When you give it to them, you grant them access to your bank account.

Protecting against the Asset Recovery Dotcon

The sure-fire way to protect yourself against a fraudulent "Asset Recovery" scheme is to try to recover the asset yourself before you commit to any company–legal or not. *Regardless of the legalese in the e-mail, you are under no obligation to contract with the Asset Recovery company just because they advised you of the unclaimed asset.*

In fact, you shouldn't. At least not until you've taken a few steps on your own. This will not only protect you from an out-and-out fraud, but it may also save you the commission due a legitimate company.

Before you sign anything then, *your strategy should be to find out as much as you can about the asset, while revealing as little as you can about yourself.*

1. Reply to the e-mail with questions–not answers. Find out about the company and how they found out about the personal data they included in their e-mail to you.

2. Try to determine the type of benefit or payment that could be involved, the date on which the payment was expected, and how the payment should have been made, which government agency is holding it, and how long it has been in escheat. A legitimate Asset Recovery will answer your questions to try to win your business; although they may be reluctant to reveal the information. An illegitimate Dotcon won't even bother to answer. They'll drop you like a hot potato.

3. Do not confirm any assertions made by the company or provide any other personal information. If the Asset Recovery company really did get the information from an asset held by the government, they can confirm it in other ways. Your disclosure of even more information at this point only increases your risk.

4. Research the asset yourself. Use the information provided by the company about the type of the asset to contact the following agencies. They should be happy to hear from you. It's their job to find you.

Uncashed money orders	US Postal Service
Unredeemed Savings Bonds	-Bureau of Public Debt
Unclaimed Social Security	-Social Security Admin
Tax Refunds	-IRS and State
Trust Funds	-Bureau of Indian Affairs Unclaimed Deposits
Unpaid Retirement	-Pension Benefit Guarantee
Mortgage Refunds	-HUD
Bankruptcy Credits	-Federal Bankruptcy Court
Lost Securities	-Securities & Exchange Comm.

5. Check the web-site for the National Association of Unclaimed Property Administrators, www.unclaimed.org. This is a non-profit organization of state officials who are responsible for returning unclaimed property to rightful owners.

TRAVEL

The rapid growth of air travel has produced a complex array of options for airports, destinations, departure and arrival times, connections and carriers. Until recently the best way for a consumer to sort out these options has been to use the services of a travel agent. The Internet now challenges this medium. Using new online travel services, you can now do just about everything a travel agent can do—faster and cheaper.

But you can't necessarily do it safer or more reliably! Like other Internet services, there are risks associated with buying from anonymous sources. You are protected from fraud if you're dealing with a licensed travel agent or the commercial carrier itself. You have legal recourse. The American Society of Travel Agents regulates the travel industry.

This is not true when contracting for travel over the Internet. Arranging travel on the Internet is more risky because you're probably not dealing with a licensed agent. When you buy a travel package online, there is no way to be sure what you're getting.

The first exposure that most of have with Travel Fraud on the Internet is Spam with the subject line of "Fabulous Travel Bargains." The first thing you should recognize is that the email message didn't come from a travel agent. More likely, it came from an individual.

The second thing you should know is that the individual probably isn't selling tickets—he's selling travel vouchers, packages, frequent flier miles, or some other medium that may or may not be redeemable for tickets, meals, or lodging according to the conditions governing their usage.

The American Society of Travel Agents prohibits the sale of these travel "substitutes" as a part of its code of ethics. They do so for a reason—to discourage fraud. The Internet has no such ethical constraints.

Transferable Tickets

One common Dotcon arriving in your mailbox is from a Dotcon artist claiming that he bought a nonrefundable but transferable ticket and can't use it. We've all been there, so we believe him when he says that he wants to sell the ticket cheap. The offer catches your attention, because it's from your local airport to a desirable location on a holiday coming up. And you know that it's legitimate because he's even got the flight number. You send the money, but you never get the ticket. The e-mail address was faked. The phone is disconnected. But it seemed so real!

Remember when you entered your home city to get free e-mail? The Dotcon artist has a targeted mailing list, and he's got the flight schedules for different cities. He never had a ticket.

Frequent flyer miles

If you've flown for a while, you probably have a pretty good idea of the comparative value of frequent flyer miles on different airlines. You can't buy or swap frequent flyer miles from licensed travel agents, so you can understand somebody else wanting to get value out of theirs. After all, you can spot a bargain when you see it.

In this Dotcon, the artist sets up an auction, telling you he's got a certain number of frequent flyer miles with a specific airline and they are about to expire. He offers to buy a ticket using the miles for the best offer. You bid a relative pittance...and he takes it!

With a mixture of elation and trepidation, you e-mail him the dates and destination of the ticket you want, and you're happy when he sends an e-mail back confirming your trip, telling you that he'll send the ticket after he gets your payment.

You charge it, and he tells you that you should receive the ticket in a few days. But you don't! You are understandably hesitant to call the airline, because you were trying to pull a fast one, so you e-mail the Dotcon artist.

He apologizes profusely for the delay and tells you that he JUST found out that the airline won't transfer miles that way, and that he'll refund your money. You never receive a refund, and your email messages bounce back.

Expiring Travel Vouchers

This is a version of the Advance Fee Dotcon involving the discounted sale of a "Fabulous Vacation" from a "travel agency.". It's an electronic version of ads you've seen in the Travel section of the Sunday paper. The Dotcon artist sends a Spam offering a bargain price on a vacation consisting of airfare and hotel. His story is that he either bought it or won it, but his wife is sick and the vacation is about to expire. It's worth several thousand dollars, but you can buy it for a couple hundred.

You bite and get an official looking vacation certificate and a travel voucher that are redeemable for a the vacation anytime before the expiration date. A few weeks later, you try to book the vacation, and the "agent" tells you their reserved slots are filled on that date. The process continues, the expiration date arrives, and your vouchers are no longer valid,

A similar Dotcon simply avoids the whole problem by selling you a travel voucher that you can't take for two months, and collecting your money in advance. The deadline for disputing a credit card charge is 60 days.

Protecting yourself against Travel Dotcons

Be skeptical if you see a web-site or get an e-mail offering you a free or bargain travel package, especially if the price seems completely unreasonable. These are some of the things you should look out for:

- Get the offer in writing. The Dotcon artist could change the offer on the web-site.
- Get the times, dates, and reservations before you pay. Travel prices change radically during the season.
- If it is an open offer, be sure there is no expiration date.
- Contact the airline and confirm the transferability of frequent flier miles and or any expiration dates
- Make sure the written information includes the price of the package plus any additional charges.
- Find out exactly what is included in the package price and what isn't.
- Get the names of specific hotels, airports, airlines and restaurants that are a part of the package. Contact them yourself to confirm.
- Check prices with local travel agencies. They may be better or more reliable.
- If the package involves standby or waitlist travel, or a reservation that can only be provided much later, get a refund statement in writing so you can cancel it.
- If you are told that you've won a free vacation, ask if you have to buy something else in order to get it. Some packages have promoted free air fare, as long as you buy expensive hotel arrangements. Others include a free hotel stay, but no air fare.
- Pay by credit card, so that you can get a credit if promised services aren't delivered.

Off-Shore Frauds

"In 1999, the SEC caught a company soliciting investments over the Internet to finance the construction of an ethanol plant in the Dominican Republic. They promised a return of 50% or more with no reasonable basis for the prediction, and the e-mails contained lies about contracts with well known companies."

The world-wide scope of the Internet promises a new dimension in the conduct of international trade. With a direct link from manufacturer to buyer, products made in one country can be marketed to consumers in another without the need for international distributors. But to realize the potential of international e-commerce, both products and money must be able to cross international borders as easily as e-mail. Unfortunately, the laws governing these transactions are unclear.

Legal Jurisdiction

Even though U.S. laws don't apply in foreign countries, it has never been easy to defraud U.S. citizens from a foreign location. The cost of international phone-calls, federal laws governing telephone marketing, and U.S. Customs made it difficult to buy and sell products across U.S. borders. The Internet has removed many of these obstacles.

A seller and buyer on the Internet are covered by state law if they both reside in the same state. They're also covered by federal law if the transaction crosses state boundaries, and they're covered by international law if it crosses borders, but these laws have not kept pace with the rapid evolution of technology. What is legal in one jurisdiction may be illegal in another, and both may claim the right to tax the proceeds of the sale.

If you purchase something from a foreign source, it may be legal for you to buy it, but illegal for the seller to sell it, or vice versa. In some cases, the transaction may be legal in both jurisdictions, but the process of delivering it or paying for it across state or national borders may be illegal. But in all cases, you must realize that you are not protected by U.S. law from fraudulent web-sites that are operated from foreign locations.

Fraud from Abroad

If you are defrauded by someone in a foreign country, the federal government can't get your money back. It's also unlikely that law enforcement officials in the foreign country will take action against the perpetrator based on your complaint. They're busy protecting their own citizens.

Some web-sites operate profitably and safely from foreign locations with this in mind. They set up just outside of the borders of the United States and market primarily to U.S. citizens. These have been named "Off-Shore" sites after the name for banks that have done the same thing for years to protect the identity of their clients and their transactions.

Other web-sites operate from foreign locations for a different reason–to escape prosecution for fraud. Sometimes it's difficult to tell which is which.

Quickie Divorces

Off-shore web-sites offer divorces in Costa Rica, the Dominican Republic and other foreign locations without either party having to reside there, or even visit. *This is not illegal, but it may be ineffective!*

Divorce is a matter for the states, not the federal government. Time was that a divorce in one state could be contested in another. But times have changed. It is possible that even a divorce granted in the Dominican Republic could stand up in court. And it is probable that a divorce granted by a foreign country is legal in the country itself, even though the parties don't reside there.

Whether it is legal in the United States, or even in some particular state, is another matter indeed. Whether or not the "Quickie Divorce" is a Dotcon then is open for question.

You may get exactly what you pay for. Whether it will be of value to you is doubtful. The best idea would be to check your state Attorney General to see if the divorce would be honored by your state before you pay for it.

Prescription Drugs

This Dotcon becomes possible because the purchase of unapproved prescription drugs from outside the company is illegal. If they're not delivered, you have no way to get your money. Purchasing prescription drugs from off-shore web-sites is also a question of safety and frugality. The conventional wisdom says *"No, they're dangerous and illegal. You don't know what you're getting, and it's probably against the law to get it."* But your bank balance says *"Yes, they're a fraction of the price of what it costs me at the corner pharmacy!"*

This dichotomy may be theoretical to the Attorney General and the Food and Drug Administration, but it is a matter of life and death to millions of senior citizens who must have these drugs to preserve their health, life, and quality of living. The price of prescription drugs in the United States is far more than any civilized nation, and the lack of coverage by Medicare drives thousands of senior citizens across the Canadian and Mexican borders in busloads to buy prescription drugs at a fraction of the cost it would cost them in the States.

The FDA would have you believe that they are inferior and dangerous, but the fact is that the quality of these "foreign versions" of prescription drugs is unknown.

Because the FDA has made the purchase of unapproved drugs illegal, the possibility arises for a Dotcon based upon the purchase of illegal products with cash in advance.

The Dotcon is evident when you must pay for the product in cash so that a credit card or check can't be traced. *If the product doesn't arrive, you have no legal recourse!* You certainly can't complain to the authorities when you don't get the item or you find that it's not really the drug you ordered. The situation is compounded when the cash went to a foreign country.

Immigration Documents

> *"On February 7, 2000, a man was convicted in California for his role in an Internet scheme that offered immigration assistance to aliens seeking to become residents or citizens of the United States."*

Just as Dotcon artists work "off-shore" to defraud us, they also work in the comfort of their homes to defraud people in other countries—whose laws don't apply to us. Immigration fraud is one of the most blatant examples.

Dotcon web-sites operated in the U.S. and off-shore offer immigration services to aliens—fake documents, transportation, contacts and the like. They charge thousands of dollars in advance for their services. In some cases, the client gets counterfeit or false immigration documents; in other cases, nothing at all. When the client complains, the Dotcon artists blame the government and the legal system for the delay in providing the promised documents.

If these services are delivered, the scheme can be prosecuted by the Customs Service as a felony–if they aren't, it's merely false advertising, a civil offense.

Online Gambling

Statistics concerning fraud in online gambling are not available, because online gambling is illegal. Nevertheless, search for "Gambling" on the Internet. You'll find hundreds of electronic casinos offering table games and sports betting. All of these sites are located in foreign countries. They have American-sounding names and are located just "offshore" in places like Saint Kitts and Antiqua. Many would put these web-sites in the same category as the investment and franchise Dotcons. They're not. For the most part, these online casinos are reputable web-sites conducting an honest business that is legal where they are, and illegal where you are.

Gambling in the United States is illegal or carefully controlled in every state but Nevada, but according to a recent report by the federal Commission on the Review of the National Policy Toward Gambling, two-thirds of all Americans have gambled. Rarely does a consumer who is defrauded while he thinks he himself is committing a crime report that fact to a law enforcement agency.

The danger to you, the consumer, is not that what you are doing is illegal; rather, it is that you will lose your money doing it. Online gambling sites require you to maintain a minimum account balance. Because they are operating outside of the jurisdiction of U.S. laws, there is little you can do to get your money back if they simply close shop and keep your money.

Electronic cash

Gold was the currency of the western frontier. Electronic cash operating from off-shore locations promises to be the currency of the new frontier of e-commerce. Electronic cash or "digital money" is a use of numbers to represent national currency rather than the bills and coins themselves. The digital money is easily converted and transferred back and forth through a computer system without the actual flow of money. Some systems are untraceable.

Because electronic cash systems can be fast, efficient, accurate, and secure, several privately owned companies have emerged to provide Internet vendors and buyers with the ability to buy and sell products and services using some variation of electronic cash. They purport to be safe and secure, and in many cases they are absolutely right.

> *Your money might well be more secure as an electronic cash number than your credit-card number floating around in clear text over the Internet. But the federal government won't insure it.*

E-cash accounts, unlike bank accounts, are not insured by the Federal Deposit Insurance Company (FDIC). If the Federal Reserve doesn't print it, the FDIC won't insure it, and the FBI can't protect you as well.

The problem is that E-cash systems are run by private companies, not the Treasury Department, so the federal government isn't responsible for keeping it safe. You go to jail if you try to pass an ink-jet replica of a fifty dollar bill. You only get sued if you defraud an E-cash company.

Anonymous E-Cash

There is a plus side to the limited federal supervision. There is more anonymity associated with E-cash transactions than with other financial transactions. Because the E-cash companies are not insured by the FDIC, the federal reporting requirements for large deposits and withdrawals are less than those found at your local bank. This provides a certain level of anonymity in and of itself.

But some of the E-cash systems advertise an additional level of privacy–offering a system that guarantees your name will not be associated with your account balance. The Treasury Department is justifiably concerned that this anonymity may be used intentionally by criminals, and unintentionally by innocent users of the system.

For example, money made from online gambling activities might be represented by E-cash with no obligation to report to the U.S. Treasury Department so a normal citizen could avoid taxes. Similarly the hidden income could be used to purchase expensive items from foreign source thereby disguising the nature and source of the income itself.

All three are a crime, and e-commerce on the Internet is going to increase the incidence of this crime. By its nature, e-commerce must make it easy and safe for money to cross borders in order for people to buy and sell things without fear of criminal prosecution. The easier it become to make secure financial transactions on the net, the more common will be the incidence of crime and fraud.

Long Distance Phone Charges

The "809" scam blatantly survives in spite of thousands of complaints and victims. The "809" area code is a "pay-per-call" number in the Caribbean like a "900" number in the states. When you dial "1-809-xxx-xxxx" to make the call, no international codes are required and you don't know you're being charged by the minute–sometimes as much as $25 per minute.

You receive a personally addressed Spam telling you to call an 809 number immediately to avoid a law-suit, rescue a relative, win a prize, or some equally persuasive motive. The phone answers right away, and someone with a Caribbean accent tries to keep you on the phone as long as possible by putting you on hold or asking questions. After ten minutes or so you hang up or are cut off.

You won't find out about this Dotcon until your phone bill arrives, and you may not have much luck getting credit for the calls, because you must resolve the problem with an international phone company.

INTERNET FRAUDS ON BUSINESSES

The word "E-commerce" was coined in the last decade of the 20th century. Today it's not just a word, it's a revolution in the way we will do business in the 21st century. The world-wide scope and lightning speed of transactions on the Internet have opened the doors for creative entrepreneurs to expand the possibilities for business and the consumer. Unfortunately the doors are also open for creative thieves to steal from legitimate businesses.

Commerce Vs. E-commerce

Internet businesses of all kinds have eased the transition of wary consumers from commerce to e-commerce by electronically replicating the things we do when we conduct business. We "visit" web-sites like we "visit" stores; we put things in an electronic shopping carts; we check out, and we electronically hand the merchant our credit card, or sometimes we pay in "e-cash".

Taking comfort in the familiarity of this process may be dangerous for both the business and the consumer. Neither can tell who they are dealing with, and both can disappear with a click of a mouse after the transaction.

The inherent speed and potential for anonymity lends itself to deception and fraud on both sides of a business transaction, and if you are conducting business on the Internet, you're going to run into your share of hackers and Dotcon artists who can play havoc with your legitimate business activities.

Business Losses

In the fall of 2000, the Federal Trade Commission estimated that fraud, security violations and thefts of intellectual property cost businesses and consumer more than a quarter of a billion dollars. This estimate is low. On August 23rd of 2000, a single fraud perpetrated by a disgruntled employee temporarily reduced the capital value of a business by $2 Billion in 15 minutes.

Identity Theft and Credit Card Fraud

The most prevalent fraud perpetrated on businesses is the fraudulent use of a credit card and personal information to purchase expensive goods or services. Although consumers themselves have only a limited liability if their credit card is misused, businesses have no such protection. Merchants who unwittingly take stolen credit card information as payment are at risk of not getting credited for the sale by credit card companies. As a merchant, you learn of this fraud well after it occurs. Such is the nature of the crime.

1. A Dotcon consumer will order an expensive product from your web-site using a name, credit card number, expiration date, and billing address he has obtained from someone else—most likely from his own Dotcon web-site.

2. He will enter a different shipping address, or call later to say he moved since he ordered the credit card or the card is his business address, and he wants it shipped to his home, or vice versa.

3. You ship the product. A month later you get a call from an angry cardholder accusing you of fraudulently making charges on his card and threatening to call the FTC unless you immediately credit his card with the amount of the purchase.

4. What do you do? The phone call itself could be a scam! Most likely, you honor the angry cardholder's complaint and set about finding the criminal. You have a fake name, fake billing address, fake phone number, but a real e-mail address and shipping address.

5. You try the e-mail first. Much to your dismay, you find that the e-mail address belongs to the legitimate cardholder! How did that happen?

The criminal used a free e-mail service to open an e-mail account in the legitimate cardholder's name.

You call the police in the town where you shipped the product to, and are informed that the shipping address was a maildrop. Then you call the maildrop and find that the box was opened in the legitimate cardholders name. Even with authorization and approval from your merchant account vendor, you take the hit.

The identity thief profits from this crime by using someone else's credit card information to purchase expensive items that can be easily resold or fenced. He gets away with the crime on the Internet, because you can't tell who he is–either before or after the crime

Protecting against frauds by identity thieves is fundamentally a matter of reducing their perceived anonymity before you close the sale of expensive items.

The Internet makes it almost impossible to completely stop a clever identity thief, because you aren't dealing with him or her in person. *But just making it risky for the Identity Thief to perpetrate the fraud for expensive items may be enough to drive him to another site. Eventually he'll find someone who hasn't read this book.*

• Post a prominent warning on your web-site stating that the fraudulent use of credit cards during interstate commerce is a federal offense and that your company will prosecute offenders to the fullest extend of the law.

- Set your web-site up to capture the buyer's e-mail address and screen orders that come from free e-mail services where the buyer can maintain an anonymous name.
- Get as much information concerning the applicant as possible for the online sale of expensive items. Be sure to get a full address and home phone number.
- Verify the billing address with the merchant vendor before authorizing the purchase.
- Call the phone number to confirm the sale.
- Require a hard-copy confirmation by fax for the shipping of expensive items to addresses that are different from the billing address on the credit card.
- Validate international orders with an additional credit reference.
- If anything seems strange after the shipment of an expensive item, call your merchant credit processor and inform them of the situation. They may have corollary information.

Employee Risks

Financial losses are not the only way the Dotcon artists can damage a business. Some may be working for you!

The advent of the Internet on every employee's desk presents a major problem to employee productivity—surfing the net for sports, games, online gambling, and even porn. In an eternal game of cat-and-mouse, employers report catching employee's wasting hours, even days, of the work week using the Internet for recreation on company time.

Disgruntled employees can also use the Internet to destroy your competitive advantage by leaking information to your competitors, ruin your brand name, libel your employees, disrupt your work force, call in the

IRS, frame you for a crime, or wipe out your business records—just to get even.

Whether you're dealing with a goof-off or a an unhappy Dotcon artist, the Internet compounds the problems you already have. These are some of the things you can do about it:

Computer Usage Policy

The first step is to produce an Computer Usage Policy for your company and have all your employees sign it, indicating that they understand and will comply.

As an employer you should ensure that the Computer Usage Policy is legally enforceable, either by using a recommended one, or having it drawn up by your legal representative. This not only defines exactly what you expect to happen, but it also gives you legal justification for terminating employees who violate the directives within.

Although the precise legal wording will differ, you should describe clearly the computer equipment, supplies and peripherals that belong to the company and direct that they be used only for company business.

According to the severity of the problem, you could specifically prohibit the use of the Internet for any purpose other than business.

You might also choose to specify that employees' e-mail is not private, and that as an employer, you can legally read e-mails coming in and out of your company. Whether or not you do so is up to you, but the statement that you have the right to protects you legally and removes any residual doubt in the employees' minds.

Refer employees to your company non-disclosure agreement (on include one in the Computer Usage Policy) and state that employees will be held liable for the release of confidential information to third parties.

Prohibit your employees from posting company information on newsgroups. Employees unknowingly leak information about your company's new products and plans.

State that you will monitor the effectiveness of the Computer Usage Policy through random sampling of e-mail, cookies, and URL selection histories without the employee's knowledge.

Configuration of Computers

After you have established a Computer Usage Policy, the best way to protect against fraud is to configure your company's computers in a standard way that protects your hardware and helps the employees comply with the policy.

It goes without saying that you should first take measures to prevent the inadvertent loss of your data from environmental factors. If you haven't done so, install power surge electrical outlets and UPS power strips.

Then install the same virus protection software program on everybody's computer and keep it updated. The danger of a viruses compounds with the number of employees using computers—even if you do not have a network. Many small offices still use the "rubber sole network". Passing floppy disks around invites viruses worse than downloading programs from the Internet.

While you're standardizing, you might install the same version of the same browser on everybody's computer and keep it updated. This will undoubtedly inconvenience some employees who are used to working with a different browser; however, it's worth it in the long run. Different versions have different bugs and are susceptible to different viruses. Some older browsers even allow unauthorized users to capture the information from your employees' hard disks while they are using the Internet.

Next configure the e-mail systems to filter unsolicited e-mail and direct it to a specific directory that only you have access to. This will not only save your employees time, but it will also provide you insight as to the attempts by strangers to contact members of your company.

You may also wish to install software that will disabuse your employees of the notion of violating the Computer Usage Policy. For example, most time-wasting is spent with e-mail, stocks, sports, games and even pornography. Installing "site blocker" software makes it difficult for employees to access these sites.

Lastly, go through all the employees' computers and delete software that your company did not purchase. If you are using pirated software, you are violating the publisher's rights and are liable for stiff penalties, if this can be proven in court. Try to get a hard copy listing of the files on the computer, and have the employee assume responsibility for any other licensed programs. This way, you are protected from liability for well-intentioned employees using pirated accidentally, unethical employees using it intentionally, and disgruntled employees reporting you to the authorities for encouraging or tolerating its use.

Industrial Security

Confidential data has value in the Information Age. If your competitor steals it, he gains a competitive edge. The Internet has significantly increased the opportunity for industrial espionage, and the Internet on everybody's desk has aggravated it even more. A complete industrial security plan is beyond the scope of this book. Before you take any action, buy any software, or hire any consultants, the first thing you should do is to find out just what everybody already knows about you and your company on the Internet.

Review your web-site for information that doesn't need to be there. The "computer guru" who built your web-site wanted to have as much content as possible. Look at the web-site from the viewpoint of your competitor. Does it reveal information that you'd rather not broadcast to the world? Even worse, does it reveal personal information about you or your employees?

Run a search on your company by name, as well as your officers, and then search for the products and services you provide. Then check the newsgroups that pertain to your company, or its products, services, or personnel to see what your company looks like to the outside world. This is exactly what a new competitor would do sometime before he completes his business plan.

Disgruntled Employees

Computer networks have provided a new way for employees to "get even!" Some employers claim this to be a major personnel problem—one that impacts not only the business, but also the personal lives of the management.

The problem frequently occurs when employees have access to the Internet without having signed a non-disclosure agreement or agreed to a similar clause in the Computer Usage Policy. "Whistleblowers" are protected by law, but rumor mongers and liars are not protected from charges of libel and slander.

When a disgruntled employee posts a nasty comment in a chatroom or an e-mail, it can affect you in several ways: it can not only damage your personal reputation or your company's, but it can also subject you to the libel charges of a third party. You may be liable for the libel because they work for you.

Employees also seek revenge on other employees by sending e-mail messages from other employee's computers—even yours. This practice can hurt the person whose computer is used as well as the person who is libeled. In a recent instance, an employee was fired for forwarding a dirty joke. It was later determined that the employee was not in his office on the date and time the message was forwarded. Someone else had simply read the joke, clicked the mouse, and forwarded it to everybody in his "friend's" address book.

Anonymity is the friend of the disgruntled employee who wants to get even with you or your company. To prevent this from happening, your Computer Usage Policy should instruct your employees to log-off when they leave their offices and to change their passwords monthly.

The disgruntled employee who has recently been terminated or quit is a special case. Cases have been reported of departing employees stealing confidential databases, pirating company software, deleting files, or planting time-bombs.

The latter is particularly ugly, and relatively simple to do for even a novice in computer programming. He merely sets up a program that activates on a specific time and date–deleting crucial company files and then the program itself. Because the tracks are hidden, and the event occurs well after the employee and others have left the company, it is difficult to determine the culprit.

To minimize the threat of a disgruntled employee seeking revenge, when you have to fire an employee under unpleasant conditions, do it on a Monday–after you've confiscated his computer and changed everybody's passwords the weekend before.

Trademark Protection

Your business name and the names of your products and services may be trademarked and protected by U.S. law, but remember the Internet is worldwide. Foreign companies can easily pilfer your names, and set up a web-site as professional as yours.

You should register all variations of the domain name for your company, and its products–before somebody else does. If you are operating a popular web-site with lots of traffic from the domain "AnySillyName.com", you can be sure that a name squatter will register "AnySillyName.net", and "AnySillyName.org" and then try to sell the rights to you! Same with the names of your products and services.

Denial of Service Dotcons

When your business depends upon the Internet, losing your Internet Service Provider (ISP)can often be fatal. This could very likely happen if the volume of hits from your website is enough to tax your ISP to the degree that he simply can't handle you any more. There are no set time limits or volume in most contracts, and continued service is based upon the relationship between your business and his.

There are new tactics in the warfare of the Information Age. A talented hacker could make your life miserable with a simple program written in Visual Basic. He can set up a battery of computers that will make requests of your server in a volume that may bring your service to a slow and agonizing halt. This results in a Denial of Service and shut-down of the website and probably your e-mail as well.

Loan Brokers

Every business needs money to expand, and probably yours is no exception, and you may turn to the Internet to find a "Loan Broker" . If you do, you should consider that some of the very professional looking web-sites you visit may disguise a Dotcon. You should be suspicious of those that require you to pay in advance for the loan, because you don't know who you are dealing with.

Most reputable loan brokers will agree to take their fee out of the loan itself—as a "finders fee". Those who have no intention, or little chance, of ever finding you a loan will want the money up-front. The Dotcon website may take you through the application form with not an indication of an advance fee until you are ready to agree to the terms of the contract. And then a small fee is required for the broker to prepare a business plan and present it to prospective investors. If you volunteer your business plan, the broker rejects it with a courteous implication that your plan was not "up to the standards" required for him to get the capital or loan.

You agree to pay the fee; the "broker" delivers the business plan, and you write him a check for several thousand dollars. Several weeks later, he reports that he has been unable to find a lender.

In fact, he made no effort to find funds as promised. You receives no loan or capital, lose advance fees paid to the broker, and have no legal recourse.

Avoiding Litigation

With unencrypted files being routinely downloaded all over the world, the Internet is a fertile ground for both intentional and unintentional copyright violations by your employees. Billion dollar Internet companies are passing confidential information around like pennies, and the law is just evolving for this new very profitable area of litigation. With deep pockets involved, it seems only a matter of time before this litigation affects your business, one way or another.

The first place to check for copyright violations is your web-site. Why? Because this is the first place your competitor will look to see if you are using graphics that belong to someone else, or plagiarized copy. If you are, it's likely that you are unaware of it.

Most likely you had the web-site created by your "computer guru"–probably a technician who has little knowledge or concern for the intricacies of intellectual property law. But whether a copyright violation is deliberate or unintentional, you can be sure that a rapacious lawyer will someday contact you.

Have a third party assess your site, another computer literate employee or firm. Check the source of pictures that you've never seen before, copy that you've never read.

Report scam artists to the Federal Trade Commission or Securities and Exchange Commission. These government agencies treat Internet crimes seriously and have prosecuted many cases.

Appendix

To find more assistance or report fraud on the Internet, visit these web-sites:

Better Business Bureau	www.bbb.org
Customs Service	www.customs.ustreas.gov
Department of Justice	www.cybercrime.gov
Federal Bureau of Investigation	www.fbi.gov
Federal Trade Commission	www.ftc.gov
Internet Fraud Complaint Center	www.ifccfbi.gov
National Attorneys General	www.naag.org
National Association of Securities Dealers	www.nasdr.com
North American Securities Administrators	www.nasaa.org
Postal Inspection Service	new.sps.com
Secret Service	www.treas.gov/usss
Securities and Exchange Commission	www.sec.gov
Sentencing Commission	www.ussc.gov
Washington State Attorney General	www.wa.gov

To contact your State Attorney General by Registered Mail:

Attorney General
State of Alabama

11 South Union St.
Montgomery AL 36103

Attorney General
State of Alaska
State Capitol
PO Box 110300
Juneau AK 99811-0300

Attorney General
State of Arizona
1275 W Washington St.
Phoenix AZ 85007

Attorney General
State ofArkansas
Tower Building
323 Center St.
Little Rock AR 72201-2610

Attorney General
State of California
1515 K St.
Sacramento CA 95814

Attorney General
State of Colorado
Department of Law
1525 Sherman St.
Denver CO 80203

Attorney General
State of Connecticut
55 Elm St.
Hartford CT 06106

Attorney General
State of Delaware
Carvel State Office Building
820 N French St.
Wilmington DE 19801

Office of the Corporation Counsel
District of Columbia
414 4th St. NW
Washington DC 20001

Attorney General
State of Florida
The Capitol, PL 01
Tallahassee FL 32399-1050

Attorney General
State of Georgia
40 Capitol Square SW
Atlanta GA 30334-1300

Attorney General
State of Hawaii
425 Queen St.
Honolulu HI 96813

Attorney General
State of Idaho
PO Box 83720
Boise ID 83720-0010

Attorney General
State of Illinois
J.R. Thompson Center
100 W Randolph St.
Chicago IL 60601

Attorney General
State of Indiana
219 State House
Indianapolis IN 46204

Attorney General
State of Iowa
Hoover State Office Building
Des Moines IA 50319

Attorney General
State of Kansas
Judicial Building
301 W 10th St.
Topeka KS 66612-1597

Attorney General
Commonwealth of Kentucky
State Capitol, Room 116
Frankfort KY 40601

Attorney General
State of Louisiana
Department of Justice
PO Box 94005
Baton Rouge LA 70804-4095

Attorney General
State of Maine
State House Building
Augusta ME 04333

Attorney General
State of Maryland
200 Saint Paul Place
CENTER>Baltimore MD 21202-2202

Attorney General
Commonwealth of Massachusetts
1 Ashburton Place
Boston MA 02108-1698

Attorney General
State of Michigan
PO Box 30212
525 W Ottawa Street
Lansing MI 48909-0212

Attorney General
State of Minnesota
State Capitol
Suite 102
St. Paul MN 55155

Attorney General
State of Mississippi
Department of Justice
PO Box 220
Jackson MS 39205-0220

Attorney General
State of Missouri
Supreme Court Building
207 W High St.
Jefferson City MO 65102

Attorney General
State of Montana
Justice Building
215 N. Sanders
Helena MT 59620-1401

Attorney General
State of Nebraska
State Capitol
PO Box 98920
Lincoln NE 68509

Attorney General
State of New Hampshire
State House Annex
25 Capitol St.
Concord NH 03301-6397

Attorney General
State of New Jersey

Richard J. Hughes Justice Complex
25 Market St. CN 080
Trenton NJ 08625

Attorney General
State of New Mexico
PO Drawer 1508
Santa Fe NM 87504-1508

Attorney General
State of New York
120 Broadway
New York NY 10271

Attorney General
State of North Carolina
Department of Justice
PO Box 629
Raleigh NC 27602-0629
Attorney General
State of North Dakota
State Capitol
600 East Boulevard Ave.
Bismarck ND 58505-0040

Attorney General
State of Ohio
State Office Tower
30 East Broad St.
Columbus OH 43266-0410

Attorney General
State of Oklahoma
State Capitol
2300 N Lincoln Blvd., Room 112
Oklahoma City OK 73105

Attorney General
State of Oregon
Justice Building
1162 Court St. NE
Salem OR 97310

Attorney General
Commonwealth of Pennsylvania
Strawberry Square
Harrisburg PA 17120

Attorney General
State of Rhode Island
72 Pine St.
Providence RI 02903

Attorney General
State of Vermont
109 State Street
Montpelier VT 05609-1001

Attorney General
Commonwealth of Virginia
Supreme Court Building
101 North Eighth Street, 5th Floor
Richmond VA 23219

Attorney General
State of Tennessee
450 James Robertson Parkway
Nashville TN 37243-0495

Attorney General
State of Texas
Capitol Station
PO Box 12548
Austin TX 78711-2548

Attorney General
State of Utah
State Office Building
Salt Lake City UT 84114

Attorney General
State of Washington
PO Box 40100
905 Plum Street, Building 3
Olympia WA 98504-0100

Attorney General
State of West Virginia
State Capitol
Charleston WV 25305-0070

Attorney General
State of Wisconsin
State Capitol
PO Box 7857
Madison WI 53707-7857

Attorney General
State of Wyoming
State Capitol Building
Cheyenne WY 82002

ABOUT THE AUTHOR

Jim Thomes is a retired Air Force Colonel who has been involved with the Internet from its conception as a world-wide military command and control system through its evolution as the foundation of e-commerce in the 21st Century. He is now the head of an information technology company in San Diego.